M000313338

Anxiety Ruins Everything

ANXIETY
Ruins Everything

HOLLY
RIORDAN

THOUGHT
CATALOG
Books

BROOKLYN, NY

**THOUGHT
CATALOG
Books**

Copyright © 2018 by The Thought & Expression Co. All rights reserved.

Cover illustration by © Henn Kim.

Published by Thought Catalog Books, a publishing house owned by The Thought & Expression Co., Williamsburg, Brooklyn.

First edition, 2018

ISBN: 978-1945796760

Printed and bound in the United States.

10 9 8 7 6 5 4 3 2 1

Vinny, thank you for being my calmness throughout my thunderclouds of anxiety.

CONTENTS

Introduction

When I was in elementary school, I would get sick when summer vacation ended, right before the first day back to classes. Every single year. My parents thought that I was faking it because I didn't want to go. Because I wanted an excuse to stay home instead.

I legitimately thought that there was something wrong with me. I found it weird that a stomach bug hit me at the same time every year, but I figured it was allergens. Something in the air.

I didn't realize until recently that it was a product of my anxiety. Unlike physical conditions—a sprained ankle or a broken arm—it's difficult to tell when you are suffering from a mental condition. My stomach felt uneasy. My head hurt. My body shook. I felt like I was going to throw up. And that's because mental illnesses can *lead* to physical illnesses. Anxiety isn't always all in your head. It can impact your body as well.

It can make you sick to your stomach. It can confine you to your bed. It can slowly ruin your life.

Some people don't understand the intensity of anxiety. They think anxiety is a flutter in the stomach before a big presentation. They think anxiety is sweaty hands before a first date. They think anxiety is deep breathing before a life-changing interview.

They think that you only have trouble sleeping on the nights before a big meeting that could make or break your career. They think that you only have panic attacks before boarding a plane for your vacation overseas. They think that you only suffer on special occasions, that your anxiety only haunts you when there is something special to fear. They don't understand that anxiety appears in more than those milestone moments. It can follow you everywhere that you go. To school. To the supermarket. To holiday dinners. To your best friend's house. Anxiety can hit for the silliest, subtlest reason or for no reason at all. It doesn't always make sense. It isn't always logical. Your family members and friends might not understand that. They might assume that, if you wanted to, you could list out the reasons why you have been so sad lately. They might think that you have a handle on your emotions like they do, that you can control how you feel, that you can choose happiness, but that just isn't the case.

Anxiety takes away your ability to think straight. It replaces your healthy thoughts with ugliness, overthinking, and paranoia. It makes you feel like everyone hates you, like you aren't good enough, like you are going to screw up every opportunity that comes your way.

Anxiety appears in different forms for different people—no two stories line up exactly—so all I can do is share my own experience with it. And hope that it helps you feel a little less alone.

My Anxiety Causes Me To Care Too Much

I care too much about what I look like. Sometimes, I make a mess of my closet by pulling out clothing and trying on ten different outfits before I find the right one. Sometimes I spend over an hour in front of the mirror, curling my hair and applying my contour. Sometimes I snap one hundred selfies in a row to get the best angle. Sometimes I do everything within my power to look good and I still feel ugly. I still feel like everyone is going to judge me the second I walk out the door.

I care too much about how other people are feeling. I care about their happiness more than I care about my own. I could be having the time of my life at a concert, but if I have a hunch that the person next to me isn't enjoying themselves, then I will stop enjoying myself. I will worry about whether or not they wish they could leave. Whether or not they hate me for dragging them there. Whether or not they are counting down the minutes until they go home.

I care too much about exes and old friends who are no longer in my life. I search through their Facebooks and Instagrams, wondering if the passive aggressive message they wrote was directed at me. I dodge them when I run into them at stores because I can't stand the possibility of walking up to them and being cursed out or cold-shouldered. I replay interactions with them in my mind on a loop, even though the relationship is over and they should already be erased from my mind.

I care too much about whether other people consider me intelligent. I will check and double check emails before sending them to my boss so that there is no chance of including a typo or grammatical error. I will do extra research before speaking at a meeting so that I sound like I know what I'm talking about. I will stay quiet, even when I know the right answer in class, out of fear that I somehow have it wrong.

I care too much about what other people are thinking. Even if they invite me over to their house, even if they are treating me with kindness, I wonder if they are only trying to be polite. If their thoughts are the complete opposite of their words. Do they think I've overstayed my welcome? Are they going to pretend they have work early to get me to leave? Are they going to be relieved when I'm gone?

I care too much about what I post on social media. How many likes I get on pictures. How many people follow me. What people will think when they scroll through my page. I will rewrite a post twenty times before publishing it—and if it doesn't do well enough, if I am embarrassed by the lack of attention, then I will remove the post from my page, hoping that no one else will see it.

I care too much about little things that I shouldn't give a fuck about. Things that I wish I didn't give a fuck about.

Sometimes Anxiety Appears For Absolutely No Reason

Sometimes anxiety hits me out of the blue. There is no reason for it. No party to attend. No test to take. No date to go on or speech to make.

My mind randomly decides to torture me with symptoms. And I can't make them go away because I have no idea what is causing them.

My entire body feels like it is on alert. Like it is getting ready for something horrible to happen.

My hands shake. My voice shakes. My legs shake.

My chest tightens. My throat tightens. My jaw tightens.

I attempt to calm myself down with the techniques therapists on TV talk about. I try to monitor my breathing by taking a deep breath in and out. In and out. I look at myself in the mirror and tell myself that everything is fine. Nothing bad is happening. It's just a regular day.

There isn't an important meeting taking place at work. There isn't a party that I have to attend. There isn't a phone call I have to make. I should be relaxed. I should enjoy the moment because there aren't many like this.

But my body refuses to listen to reason. It gives me strong headaches. It gives me heart palpitations. It gives me the urge to vomit.

Even though there aren't any worries in my mind, my body is so used to stressing that it continues to do so. And then I end up having anxiety over the fact that I have anxiety. It creates an inescapable cycle. It makes me feel like my world is ending and I am powerless to stop it.

If someone happens to notice that I'm acting strange, I will turn the conversation back around to focus on their day instead. I will avoid talking about myself because I won't be able to explain the situation to them. Saying that I am okay is a lie—but if I admit that I am *not* okay, they will ask why.

Why? Because anxiety sucks. Because anxiety doesn't fight fair. Because anxiety is an attention whore who will *not* be ignored.

But they won't accept any of those answers. They will want to know *why* I am feeling so anxious. What have I been worrying about? What has been on my mind?

Some people don't understand how I can't understand myself. They think that I am just hiding my feelings from them because I don't trust them enough. That I'm not in the mood to talk. That I would rather shut them out than be honest.

That is why I work so hard to hide my symptoms, even from the people I love the most. I don't want them to feel like I am pushing them away. I don't want them to sit there and try to pinpoint why I'm so upset when I don't even know the reason myself. I don't want to put them through the same pain that my brain puts me through every damn day.

No One Realizes How Bad My Anxiety Actually Is

No one realizes how bad my anxiety actually is because I have my life together. Even though I struggle to hold conversations, I still have friends. Even though I have meltdowns before interviews and important meetings, I still have a career. Even though I have no control over half of the thoughts that pop into my brain, I am still doing well for myself.

No one realizes how bad my anxiety actually is because I have learned to *fake* it. I hyperventilate inside of my car before meeting a group of friends for dinner, so that I am calm by the time I get inside. I escape to the bathroom when a party becomes too hectic and then wear a fake smile after opening the door and socializing again. I am able to hold myself together in public, but the second that I am alone, I collapse.

No one realizes how bad my anxiety actually is because I hide my symptoms as best as I can. If someone happens to notice the redness on my cheeks, I will tell them that it's only because the room is too hot. Or that my allergies have been acting up. Or that I have been feeling under the weather lately. I will come up with bullshit excuses to avoid telling the truth. I will lie through my teeth if that means that I will come across as normal.

My anxiety has turned me into a skilled liar. Instead of telling my friends that I can't hang out because my anxiety is tethering me to the house, I will tell them that I have to work an extra shift. That my parents need my help with something. That I have to babysit. That I have a cold. I will find a way to get out of making plans without making them suspicious.

No one realizes how bad my anxiety actually is because I keep most of my thoughts trapped inside of my head. I avoid voicing my worries. I'll sit there in silence, thinking about all of the ways I went wrong in the past, but when someone asks me what is on my mind, I will make a joke. I will talk about something—anything—other than what I was just thinking about. I will put on a mask in front of them.

No one realizes how bad my anxiety actually is because there are times when my hands stay steady, when my voice stays calm, and when my back stays straight, but I am suffering inside. There are times when I feel like I am suffocating, but I look perfectly normal to everyone around me. There are times when my insides and my outsides are mismatched.

No one realizes how bad my anxiety actually is because it's not something I am comfortable talking about, even to my close friends and family members. I am too embarrassed to sit them down and tell them the truth. I don't want them to know how hard it is for me to act like a functioning human being. I don't want them to see how much my anxiety weighs me down.

4

I Hate How Bad I Am At Socializing

I admire the kind of people who can talk about any subject for hours at a time. The kind of people who can chitchat with complete strangers like they are old friends from high school. The kind of people who breeze through any social situation, who make speaking seem like the easiest thing in the world.

I wish that I could be more like those people. I wish that I was born with the ability to be likable.

But I suck at socializing. I cringe at the thought of getting stuck in an elevator with someone chatty or having a talkative cab driver because I am terrified they are going to keep speaking to me and will end up disappointed at my answers.

I hate how hard I struggle to hold a conversation. I never know how to respond when someone else speaks. Instead of coming up with a clever response, I either smile or laugh or nod silently. I barely contribute anything to the conversation, which is why it dies as soon as it begins.

I am sure that it looks like I couldn't care less about what they are saying. Like I wish that they would walk away and leave me alone. Like I prefer the quiet.

No one sees how much I appreciate the fact that they are talking to me at all. I want them to keep talking. I want to hear what they have to say. I have an interest in their life. I just have no idea how to convey that out loud. I have no idea how to comfort someone when they're sad or reassure someone when they're doubting themselves. I have no idea how to be a good friend or coworker or customer.

I am a good listener, but that is about as far as it goes. I suck with every other aspect of socializing.

Instead of holding eye contact with the other person, I glance toward the ground out of insecurity. Instead of speaking loudly and clearly, I mumble out of self-consciousness. Instead of going into detail about whatever I'm talking about, I keep my sentences clipped out of fear of rambling and being boring.

I wish that I had more confidence in myself. I wish that silences didn't feel so awkward. I wish that conversations didn't die so quickly. I wish that I could come up with something interesting to add instead of answering with a simple *yes* or a *no*. I wish that I could tell jokes that would make people laugh on the spot. I wish I could give compliments and tell stories that would make people like me.

I wish that I could get excited over parties that I was invited to and family gatherings with the cousins I miss instead of freaking out about how awkward I am going to look. How unapproachable I am going to seem. How out of place I am going to feel.

I wish that my mind worked differently. I wish that speaking came naturally to me. I wish that I was capable of carrying a conversation for more than a minute. I wish that I liked myself.

5

Anxiety Mixed With Depression Is Confusing AF

The two sides of my mind are in a constant state of war. My anxiety makes me feel like I am not doing enough like, I need to try harder—but my depression makes me feel like I am doing too much, like I need to slow down.

My anxiety causes me to stress about all of the things on my to-do list. The projects I have to complete. The chores I have to finish. The phone calls I have to make. But my depression convinces me to stay in bed for a little longer. To hit snooze one more time. To keep sleeping because there is no point in getting up anyway.

My anxiety makes me worry that I'm being a bad friend, that I am going to lose the people closest to me if I keep my distance from them—but my depression zaps my energy. It makes me close myself off. It convinces me to ignore texts from the people I care about, even though my anxiety is screaming at me to answer so that I don't lose their friendship forever.

My anxiety makes me nervous I will lose my job or flunk my class if I mess up one more time—but my depression tells me that I should take the day off, that I should give myself a break, that I'd be happier staying in bed. But the entire time I'm in bed, I'm suffering from FOMO. I'm thinking of what a horrible person I am for calling out sick from work or skipping class when I should be there alongside everyone else. My anxiety keeps me up, wondering whether my boss is going to use the opportunity to fire me, but my depression tells me to stay in bed anyway.

My anxiety makes me freak out about the test I have tomorrow, but my depression takes away my ability to study. It distracts me from my textbooks. It puts my mind into a fog, making me feel like I've had too much to drink. It makes it impossible for me to do the things that I know I should be doing.

My anxiety causes me to panic about what is going to happen if I don't text someone back or show up for work or go to my friend's party. The logical thing would be to do those activities so I can stop worrying, but my depression has stolen all of my ambition. It has turned me into an unmotivated, lost soul.

My anxiety is telling me that I am going to turn out to be a failure if I don't work harder, that I am going to die alone and embarrass my entire family. But my depression is telling me that it doesn't matter, that life is pointless, that there is no use in trying.

My anxiety keeps me up past midnight, worrying about death, about what will happen when the reaper arrives. And my depression already has the welcome mat out for Him.

6

Texting Activates My Anxiety

My anxiety convinces me that the people closest to me want nothing to do with me. That they're only dealing with me to be nice and secretly want me to leave them alone. That, even though I consider them a good friend, they consider me a nuisance.

My anxiety makes me write out texts and then delete them before sending. It makes me keep to myself when I am dying to talk to someone because I don't want to bother them with my petty problems and my stupid jokes and my clingy friendships.

Since I don't want to annoy anyone, I hesitate to text people first. Instead of reaching out to them, I will get upset about the lack of notifications on my screen. I will turn hypocritical and wonder why no one cares about me—because, after all, if they wanted to talk to me, they would text first, wouldn't they?

When I actually do find someone to text, I will write out the message in my notes app and then copy and paste it so the other person doesn't see those three dots appearing and disappearing as I type and erase, type and erase, attempting to create the perfect text. One that is spelled right and sounds casual, like it came off the top of my head.

If the text I send happens to be risky, I either toss my phone across the room or switch it to silent or flip it over so the screen is invisible. So I can keep fooling myself into believing that they haven't read it yet and that everything is okay. But, despite my calm-and-collected act, the fear doesn't go away when my phone does.

The second I press send, my heart will race. I won't be able to concentrate on anything other than their impending response. My mind will go through all of the possible things they could say to me. All of the ways they could curse me out or cause me to cry or make me feel small. My thoughts jump straight to the worse case scenario because I always believe something horrible will happen. That a single text has enough power to ruin my relationships, my friendships, my self-esteem.

Even if their text comes through and appears perfectly normal at first glance, I will overanalyze everything. I will wonder why they used a period instead of an exclamation point. I will freak out over how short their sentence was. I will wonder if that 'joke' they made was meant to sound sarcastic or serious.

And if they take too long to answer, that is even more stress-inducing. I will wonder if they are intentionally ignoring me or if they are only busy with work. Did I say something to make them mad? Did I bore them? Did I bother them?

If I am being completely honest with myself, it doesn't matter how slow or fast they text back. It doesn't matter if they send one word or five paragraphs. I will always overanalyze. I will always assume that they would rather be left alone than deal with someone like me.

My Anxiety Is The Worst Right Before Bed

Anxiety attacks me at midnight. It claws me to shreds after I am done scrolling through my phone and am left with my own thoughts.

While my eyes are closed and my head is snug against its pillow, I think about the mistakes that I have made throughout my life. The dumb things I did to impress someone I had a crush on. The mean words to friends that have dripped from my lips. The jokes I have told that no one laughed at and the texts I have sent that no one answered.

I think about all of the things that I have done wrong, big and small, and there isn't a time limit on them. Some of the things happened weeks ago, months ago, years ago. I am unable to let go of the memories. I am unable to move past them.

When I am not regretting my past, I am worrying about my future. I am thinking about all of the stressful things I have to do the next day. I am trying to figure out what I am going to wear and where I am going to park and what time I am going to leave. I am stressing about whether I have enough money for rent and how long I should wait to text my crush back and what I should write in the email I've been putting off sending my boss.

Some of the things I worry about aren't even logical. I create scenarios in my head that are laughable, utterly ridiculous. *What would I do if someone else sat in my seat at the lecture tomorrow? Would I be able to find another place to sit? What if I accidentally steal someone else's seat and they get pissed at me?* Deep down, I know that none of those things are ever going to happen (and would be easy to deal with if they did), but it doesn't stop me from being nervous about it.

The entire time that my mind is running through scenarios, I keep taking short breaks to glance at my clock, counting down the hours until I have to wake up in the morning. The more time that passes, the more anxious I get, because *I am not going to get enough sleep. I am going to have bags under my eyes. I am going to fall asleep at the wheel and total my car.*

My anxious thoughts haunt my mind until I pass out, and then they turn into anxious dreams. Dreams where I'm back in high school and forgot to study for a big test. Dreams where I am late for work because I keep turning down the wrong roads. Dreams where all my friends get together to admit that they can't stand me and only talk to me because they feel bad for me.

And in the morning, after I shake the bad dreams away, I'm still feeling anxious because it's time to go through the process all over again.

My Anxiety Makes Me Avoid People As Much As Possible

When my roots are showing, I will dye my hair at home instead of going to the salon because I hate making small talk with the woman scraping a brush across my scalp.

When I feel under the weather, I will look up my symptoms on my phone instead of visiting the doctor to avoid sitting inside of a waiting room elbow-to-elbow with coughing strangers.

When I have a question for customer service, I will send the company an email and wait an entire day for a response instead of making a phone call and finding out the information right away.

I will buy movie tickets online. I will buy clothes online. I will buy groceries online. Any time that I can use the internet in place of human interaction, I will do so. I love dentists who allow me to schedule my appointments online. I love companies who have a chat box on their site to text a representative. I love when there are loopholes to talking to real people face-to-face or even hearing their voice over the phone.

My anxiety makes me avoid people as much as possible. It

makes me nervous to talk to someone, even if it is their *job* to talk to me. Even though they get paid to deal with customers all day long and won't remember my face the second I leave their shop.

I will choose the self-checkout line at the grocery store even when the rest of the lines are empty. I will drive past full-service gas stations on an empty tank to find one with self-service. I would rather inconvenience myself by doing a job myself than associate with the person who is hired to do it.

I hate how illogical my fears can be. There is no reason for me to be nervous about walking up to a cashier and letting them scan my items or handing money to a gas station attendant through my window. They probably won't say more than *how are you*. I will probably never see them again. I will probably not embarrass myself. I will probably be perfectly fine.

None of that matters, though. When I'm about to enter a social situation, my thoughts aren't as clear as they sound on paper. I'm not actually thinking *I hope I don't embarrass myself in front of them*. I'm thinking *I don't want to do this, I really don't want to do this*. I can't name a reason why. I just feel that way. I just feel terrified.

That is my biggest problem with anxiety. Most of the time, it doesn't make much sense. A part of my brain can be thinking about how I don't care what those people think of me, about how there is nothing to worry about, and the other part of my brain is making my hands shake and my breathing heavy.

Those two parts of me are in constant conflict, a never-ending battle. I know that I shouldn't be nervous, but I can't help myself. I know that I am overreacting, but it happens anyway. I know that there is nothing to worry about, but worrying is all that I do.

I Even Have Anxiety Around Family…

People assume that anxiety only occurs around new people. In new places. Surrounded by the unexpected. But that is not true at all. It can occur at any time, in any place, even when I am in a room filled with people I have known since childhood, since the day I was born.

The most embarrassing kind of anxiety occurs during family parties. On Christmas. Easter. Thanksgiving. During holidays and birthday parties when I should be excited to catch up with everyone, but am filled with nerves instead.

This kind of anxiety sucks so much because I should be comfortable with these people by now. I grew up with them, I love them, so it should be easy for me to make small talk with them. It should be second nature to me.

And yet, I still struggle to tell them about what has been going on in my life. I still stutter and stumble over my words.

The fact that I can't do something as simple as talk to my own aunt or uncle or cousin makes me even more nervous. It makes me feel like even more of an outsider. Like there is something wrong with me that no one else could ever understand.

Some family members make it worse by turning my silence into a running joke. They think that they are helping by *including* me, but they only make things worse when they draw attention to me by jokingly asking *why I won't shut up*. I already realize that I am quiet, but the reminders hurt. And when I have no answer to their comment, no clever response that will make the room chuckle, I feel even more embarrassed.

That is why I usually end up shuffling around the kitchen, helping the host cook or clean to keep myself busy. Either that or I will crouch on the ground to play with the babies who can't hold a conversation yet, who can't make me feel awkward and alone yet.

If no one walks up to me while I'm doing those things, I will feel like no one wants me there. But I won't walk up to them either because my anxiety makes it hard for me to jump into conversations.

I don't want to stumble over to a group of people who have gathered together because they will probably have a better time without me. And I don't want to sit somewhere where I'm unwanted and have them silently wish that I would have chosen a different room. I don't want to ruin everyone else's fun.

Even if it is clear that they want to include me—if I'm invited to play a game of poker or basketball or beer pong—I will turn down the offer. It's because I am terrified of saying or doing something stupid, but they won't realize that. To them, it will look like I'm a snob. Like I think I'm too good for them. Like I have no interest in becoming close to them.

No one realizes how much I care about them, not even

my own family because my anxiety convinces me to keep to myself. It tricks me into thinking I am all alone in this world.

10

…And Anxiety Around My Closest Friends

There is nothing I hate more than last minute plans. I want to know what I am doing days ahead of time so I can pick out a nice outfit and take a long shower and prep myself mentally for what is about to happen.

I need to psych myself up for social interactions. I can't dive headfirst into them without doing my research. Where exactly *is* this restaurant? How long does it take to get there? What roads should I take? These are questions I always ask.

Of course, even if the plans were set in stone months earlier, that doesn't mean I can go through with them.

If my anxiety happens to act up on the day of an event, I am forced to lie about why I'm backing out, because most of my friends won't understand why I suddenly need to be alone. They will accept an excuse about being sick or getting stuck working the late shift, but they wouldn't accept the truth – that as much as I want to see them, I can't stomach the thought of dealing with people that day.

If I told them that, they would accuse me of being lazy. They would call me a flake. They would mistakenly think that I don't value their friendship, that it is a chore to be around them. And that's not true at all. It's not *them*. I love them.

If my anxiety wasn't an issue, I would spend every spare moment with them. But the truth of the matter is that there are certain places that I would rather not follow them to on weekends. I would rather hang out at someone's house than go to a bar or a club. I would rather stay in a safe place than be thrust into a crowd where we're going to be surrounded by strangers. I hate turning them down and feeling like I'm missing out on something fun, but I refuse to leave my comfort zone.

Since my anxiety makes me feel like such a bad friend, since it makes me doubt everyone's intentions, I need constant reassurance that my friends like me. I will repeatedly ask them if they're sure they want to hang out this weekend. I will ask if my texts are annoying them. I will ask if they want me to leave them alone.

It's not that I'm fishing for compliments. I just need reminders of their love, because little things will make me think that they hate me. If they post a group picture on Snapchat without me, proving that they hung out without me, I will wonder why I was excluded. There is probably an obvious reason like they knew I was working that day or they knew I wasn't interested in the concert they saw, but it still hurts. It still makes me wonder if they are trying to ease me out of the group.

No matter how many years I have been friends with someone, anxiety still makes me doubt whether or not they actually care.

Anxiety Makes Little Things Feel Like The End Of The World

I am always saying sorry because I feel like I am constantly screwing up. I apologize for texting back too fast *and* for waiting too long to text back. I apologize for showing up too late *and* for showing up too early. I apologize for talking too much *and* for not saying anything at all.

I believe that anyone who is forced to spend time with me deserves an apology for putting up with me. But since I cannot say that aloud, I come up with any excuse that I can to apologize. *Sorry that my dog keeps jumping on you. Sorry that I don't have any good food in my fridge. Sorry that the house is such a mess. Sorry that I look like such a mess.*

I apologize over the smallest things, so when something big happens, when someone is actually mad with me, I self-destruct. If someone raises their voice at me, even if they swear that they are not yelling and are not even angry, I want to burst into tears.

To me, any mistake feels like the end of the world.

If I make a mistake at work, I end up convincing myself that I will get fired. If I make someone I'm dating upset, I am convinced that they will leave me. I am convinced that the tiniest thing will make others realize that I don't deserve their time. That it will be the nudge they need to abandon me without a glance back.

My anxiety turns the most miniscule problems into apocalyptic type problems. I will come close to a meltdown if I am forced to take a detour on my drive to work. If a meeting time is changed. If I run out of the cereal I planned on eating for breakfast. If I wake up at eight instead of seven.

The change might not make much of a difference to my day, but my brain will have trouble processing it. I need stability. Routine. Predictable.

I am not the kind of person who gets excited over surprises thrown on birthdays. I am not the kind of person who can handle spontaneously hopping on a plane and jetting overseas. I am not the kind of person who can handle thinking on the fly. I need time to plan out what is going to happen tomorrow and the next day and the next week. I need the illusion of control.

I wish that I could take a road trip with my friends without needing to know the exact details about what I should wear and what I should bring and how long we're going to be out. But my anxiety makes it impossible for me to go with the flow. To act down to earth. Low maintenance. Fun.

I need structure in my life, I need answers to all of my questions, because if there is a change in plans, if things stop going the way I imagined it over and over in my head the night before, it feels like my world is crashing down around me.

Anxiety Makes Me Feel Like I Have No Friends

Anxiety makes it seem like I don't care about the people who matter the most to me because I'm terrified of coming on too strong. I don't want to compliment them and have them think I'm weird. I don't want to invite them over and get turned down. So I stay quiet instead. I let them think I don't care at all instead of letting them see I care too much.

Anxiety convinces me not to text anyone because I don't want to bother them. I don't want them to feel obligated to answer me. And after all, if they really wanted to talk to me, then they would have initiated a conversation themselves, wouldn't they? If they haven't been reaching out to me, then they must not want anything to do with me.

Anxiety makes me feel like I don't fit into any group. Like everyone else would be happier without me around. That's why I never feel guilty about canceling plans at the last second. I feel like I'm doing them a favor. Like they're secretly relieved we're not going to hang out.

Anxiety makes me stay locked inside my house, even when I'm feeling restless and want to find something exciting to do.

It convinces me that I'm safer inside of my room. That I would feel uncomfortable if I decided to go out to a restaurant or a bar because there would be too many people around to look at me. To judge me.

Anxiety stops me from flirting with anyone I'm interested in because it makes me overthink until my mind feels raw. It makes me wonder if I'm talking too much or if my face has turned red or if my outfit makes me look unattractive. Instead of having some fun talking to the person I like, it only causes me more stress.

Anxiety even stops me from joining dating apps, because the thought of talking to someone over the phone is enough to make my heart pound. I hate waiting for replies. I hate spending the time between messages wondering if I said something stupid and if the other person is going to hate me for it.

Anxiety makes me nervous to do something as simple as add someone on social media. It convinces me to lurk in group conversations so I can read everything even though I never type anything. It makes me afraid to join in because I don't want to ruin the fun.

Anxiety stops me from talking to strangers online and at the supermarket. What if I say something wrong? What if they're rude to me? Or even worse, what if that stranger is a serial killer who is going to hurt me?

Anxiety makes me overthink everything and undervalue myself.

Anxiety makes me feel like I have no friends — because it stops me from interacting with others. It stops me from reaching out to people that I love the most because I don't want to get rejected or feel awkward or embarrass myself.

Anxiety makes me feel like I'm all alone, even though I know that's not the truth.

Anxiety Even Haunts Me At Home

When I hear knocks on the door, even though I wasn't expecting any company, my entire body tenses. In all likelihood, it's only someone trying to get me to switch cable networks or convert me to their religion, but I hate telling people *no* when they refuse to accept that as an answer. I hate feeling awkward on the front stoop of my own home.

Most of the time, I will ignore the knocks, but if I'm expecting a package, I get worried it could be the delivery man because they might take my goods back to the post office if I fail to answer. Then I would have to drive down there and suffer through even *more* social interaction, which is the last thing I want to do on a lazy afternoon.

I always have the urge to peek through the curtains to see who it is, but if they caught me staring, then I would feel obligated to answer the door and have an actual conversation with them. So I choose to hide in a corner instead, shush my dog to keep him from barking and hope the mystery guest will leave soon.

It's the same with phone calls. If my phone rings instead of giving me a text notification, I lose all rational thought. If the number is unrecognizable, then I pull up a browser on my laptop and use Google to find out who the person is instead of simply answering the phone and finding out the traditional way.

Even if the call is coming from someone I am close with, from a friend or a family member, most of the time I will press ignore and then text them to ask if they called me on purpose. I will try to conduct the entire conversation over text where I can take the time to plan out my responses instead of over the phone where I have to think on the spot.

It should go without saying that I avoid phone calls whenever possible. If I can order a pizza over the company's app or schedule a doctor's appointment using an online system, then I will do so. Even if it takes more energy to log onto the right site than to make a two-minute call, I will take that route. I will inconvenience myself to avoid human interaction.

If I have no other choice but to make a call, I grab a piece of paper and jot down the exact words that I am going to say, hoping that the person on the other end of the line doesn't do something to ruin my script.

The only thing worse than phone calls is Skype calls. Even if my boss requests to speak with me for five minutes tops, it takes me a full day to make myself look presentable. To get the lighting right. To make sure that the background is free of clutter.

During the call, I don't even look at the other person. I look at the tiny version of myself in the square in the corner, silently hating how anxious I look and hoping my boss doesn't notice the nonstop fidgeting. Hoping my anxiety doesn't help me lose my job the same way it's made me lose my mind.

14

My Anxiety Makes Me Terrified Of Authority

I am terrified of authority figures. Professors. Bosses. Police officers. Security guards. Anyone who has the power to get me in trouble.

When I'm driving down the street and see a cop car perched on the side of the road, I become paranoid. My eyes flick back to the speedometer to make sure that I am going a legal speed. My hands tighten on the steering wheel as soon as I lower the blast of my radio. I become convinced that red and blue lights are going to flash behind me. I get worried that a mark will be placed on my record, that a ticket will be written out in my name.

But the police aren't my biggest issue. It doesn't matter how well I get along with my superiors at work because I am always intimidated by them. Whenever my boss wants to talk to me, I create a mental list of every little mistake that I have made since I was hired. Even if I know the conversation is going to be filled with praise, that I'm due for a raise or an annual review, I can't push away the fear in the back of my mind that I will get reprimanded. That I will unfairly get fired and lose everything I've worked so hard to earn.

My anxiety over authority figures is so bad that I freak out whenever there is the slightest chance of being confronted. It happens when I walk through a metal detector before entering a concert hall or when I walk through the exit of a grocery store. I'm terrified of those machines beeping and alerting security, even though I have done nothing wrong. Even though they could search through my bags and jean pockets and wouldn't find anything illegal.

This fear started when I was a kid. When I was still in school, I behaved the best out of all of my classmates, because I was terrified of the teacher calling me out for texting or passing notes. I didn't want everyone's eyes drawn to me. I didn't want to become the center of attention. More than that, I didn't want to deal with any confrontation.

I cannot stand conflict. I will break down in tears when someone raises their voice at me, even if they aren't saying anything inherently mean. I hate the thought of someone being angry at me, even for a split second – especially if that person has the power to give me a week of detention or take away my job or put me behind bars.

Besides, I have trouble thinking on the spot, so when someone asks me to explain myself, I never know what to say. I will stutter and stumble and appear guilty, even though it's really a product of my nervousness. It will look like I have done something wrong, even though I make a point to always play by the rules.

Authority figures freak me out because they have more power than I do. Because they can say the word and ruin my week. Because they can do whatever they want to me and I just have to deal with it.

15

My Anxiety Makes School A Living Nightmare

The stress starts early in the morning, during roll call. Instead of chitchatting with friends like the rest of the class, I pay close attention to the teacher's lips, afraid I will miss the sound of my name. Until I do, I repeat 'here' over and over again in my head, praying I will be able to say the word without my voice cracking, without drawing unwanted attention to myself.

And all throughout class, I never raise my hand, even if I am convinced I know the right answer to a question. The thought of speaking aloud and somehow embarrassing myself in front of a group of people I will be stuck with for the rest of the year is too stressful to handle.

My participation grade suffers because I hold myself back from saying what is inside of my head. My teachers believe I know less than I do because I never prove my knowledge aloud, only on written tests.

If the teacher decides to ruin my day completely by actively looking for someone to call on, claiming that they don't want to keep talking to the loud popular kids with their hands high in the air, I freak out.

I hold my water bottle to my lips to appear busy. I flip through my notes, pretending to be searching for the answer. I look up at the ceiling, down at my desk, anywhere but at the teacher, trying to telepathically beg them not to call on me.

If my mission fails, if I'm asked to speak even though that's the last thing I want, I am distracted during the rest of the class. Instead of listening to whatever the teacher rambles on about, I replay whatever I had just said in my head over and over again, wondering if I phrased it the right way or if I stumbled over my words. Wondering if anyone noticed my cheeks turning red and my breathing turning heavy.

Even if ten minutes have gone by since I've spoken, the adrenaline doesn't wear down. My body is still tense. My heart is still beating fast. I have the urge to run to the bathroom to escape, but that would mean I would have to get up and walk past a roomful of people who will judge every step I take and every piece of clothing on my body, and that sends another wave of stress through my veins.

The only thing worse than being singled out in the middle of class is being asked to form groups or separate into pairs when I have no friends. Everyone else is thrilled to make their own choice, but I would rather be matched up with someone by the teacher, so I don't have to awkwardly glance around the room for someone as alone as I am. So I don't have to admit that I have no one.

The anxiety doesn't disappear even when I'm back at home, in a place I consider safe because I always know that I'm going to have to repeat the process again the next day. And the next. And the next. All the way until graduation day.

16

What It's Like Living With Anxiety As A 20-Something

I win every game of *Never Have I Ever* that I play because I haven't experienced nearly as much as the people surrounding me. Compared to them, I am a hermit. I am a recluse. I am an outsider.

While everyone else spends their time talking face-to-face at parties and taking group pictures on trips overseas, I waste my time on the computer. My eyes are always attached to a screen.

Unlike most kids in their twenties, I have never done a keg stand. Never drank from a beer funnel. Never eaten a 'brownie'. Never smoked a cigarette.

I have never traveled on my own. Never went to the cinema on my own. Never went to dinner on my own. Never lived on my own.

I feel like I'm missing out on my younger years. Like I should be taking more risks. Meeting more people. Going more places. Seeing more sights.

I should be going to house parties, getting drunk off of my ass with people I won't remember the next morning, and regretting it all when I wake up the next day.

I should be going out on hot dates every Friday night and meeting up with my friends on Saturday for brunch to brag (or complain) about how it went.

I should be taking spontaneous road trips with my friends and uploading pictures to Instagram so everyone can comment on how jealous they are.

I should be taking off from work because I'm young and dumb and can afford to rest for one day.

I should be having more fun. I should be letting myself breathe.

But I haven't done any of those things because my anxiety keeps me glued to my bedroom. It convinces me that I should stick to my schedule of waking up, working, watching Netflix, and going back to bed.

Even though there are exciting things I want to do, items on my bucket list that are far from being crossed off, I talk myself out of them because *who would go with me? When would I have the time?*

In my head, I plan out all of the things that I want to do, but I never take the incentive to turn them into a reality. They remain as daydreams, fantasies that I can return to whenever I'm bored.

I'm the kind of person who gets annoyed when friends go out without me, even though I would have turned them down anyway. The kind of person who complains about never doing anything, but sits on my ass all day instead of making a change. The kind of person who exists instead of lives.

I feel like when I'm older, I won't have any stories to tell about the adventures I took. I won't have any pictures to look back on, other than selfies that took me twenty times to get right. I won't have any memories to make me feel like I led a successful, fulfilling life.

I feel like I am wasting my twenties. And I'm worried I'm going to waste the rest of my life as well.

17

Anxiety Follows Me To Every Party

I feel like a hypocrite because I will complain about having no friends, having no one to text when something is bothering me and no one to visit when I have a day off from work, but nine out of ten times I will turn down any invitation out. I will make up lies about how I have to work or make excuses about how I'm feeling under the weather. I will weasel my way out of a good time because I am terrified of the unknown.

The only way that I will attend a party is if I am close to someone else who is going, aside from the host. Someone who will let me follow them around all night like a puppy dog. Someone who won't mind driving there with me so I don't have to walk inside alone. Someone who will agree to leave as soon as I feel the need to escape.

If that person wanders off at some point, I will migrate toward the snack table to stuff my face with food. As long as my hands look busy, no one will realize that I am alone. As long as my mouth is full, no one will expect me to make small talk with them.

If there is a dog, I might even leave my spot by the food

to crouch onto the ground and play with him. At least, with an animal, I don't have to worry about answering questions. I don't have to worry about being judged. I can just enjoy the moment the way that 'normal' people do with each other during parties.

A few sips of alcohol might make me feel a little lighter, it might loosen my tongue and help me hold conversations with people I would normally avoid. It might give me a few hours of freedom where I can smile without being insecure about my teeth and tell jokes without analyzing how many people found them funny.

But when the vodka wears off, when I am back to my old self, I revert back to being antisocial.

Ever since I was little, it has been hard for me to be around large groups of people. Whenever I hear laughing, I assume that it's about me. I instantly become self-conscious, wondering if there is a stain on my jeans or lipstick smudged across my chin. Worrying that I am making a complete fool of myself without even knowing it.

When those toxic thoughts swarm my mind, when they overtake my common sense, I will escape to the bathroom. I will stare into the mirror and wonder what the hell is wrong with me. I will pull out my phone and text someone who can calm me down.

And, eventually, I will decide that the best thing for me to do is leave the party early. Early enough to preserve my sanity. Early enough to make everyone else question whether I hate them, whether I think that I'm too good for them. They mistake my silence for hatred when really, I'm terrified that *they* hate *me*.

18

My Anxiety Is The Real Reason Why I Suck At Flirting

No one can tell when I have a crush on them because I never show any signs of being attracted to them. I don't flip my hair back. I don't bat my eyelashes. I don't pout my lips or attempt to apply my chapstick as seductively as possible.

When I like someone, I flick my eyes away every time they meet my gaze because I am too embarrassed to look them in the eyes. I give one-word answers over text even though I would freak out if someone did the same to me. I avoid them as much as possible because I have no idea what to say to them and would rather daydream about talking to them in my head than actually go through with it in real life.

I come across like I can't stand you when I want to be with you because flirting doesn't come naturally to me. It's hard enough for me to hold a conversation with someone else my age who I have zero interest in ever seeing again – and that pressure grows ten times worse when I'm around someone I actually care about impressing.

Even though I want to text my crush first, I hold back out of fear that I won't get a response. Even though I want to sit as close to them as possible, I keep my distance in case they get angry about me invading their personal space. Even though I want to ask them to hang out one-on-one over the weekend, I act like I'm too busy to see them.

The more I like someone, the harder it is for me to communicate with them. The more I like someone, the further away I push them.

My anxiety, mixed with my boatload of insecurities, stops me from believing that anyone could develop feelings for me. If someone stares at me from across the room, instead of offering a smile and concluding that they must find me attractive, I assume I must have food in my teeth or mascara smudged down my cheek. My brain goes through all of the embarrassing reasons they could be looking my way instead of reminding me that this could be a *good* thing.

Whenever someone flirts with one of my friends, I'm the first person to notice and to point it out. But when it comes to my own love life, I am ignorant as can be.

Since I'm so socially awkward, I usually do my flirting over the internet. By sending them a picture of my dog over Snapchat. By liking all of their photos on Instagram. By posting an attractive photo of my own and hoping they'll see. By doing tiny things that seem huge to me, but my crush probably doesn't even think twice about.

No one ever knows how I feel about them because my anxiety doesn't want me to take risks. My anxiety doesn't want me to put myself out there. My anxiety wants me all to itself.

19

I Have Uncontrollable Anxiety While Driving

I get nervous driving on new roads, roads that I have never placed my wheels on before, even if my GPS is speaking to me in the background. Although it has never let me down before, I always wonder whether it is going to malfunction and send me down the wrong road. Or if it's going to lose its internet connection and leave me lost and alone.

Even when I'm familiar with the streets, I get nervous the second that someone starts to inch too close to me. I hate when my personal space is invaded, even if I'm inside of a car. I want everyone to keep their distance. I want room to breathe.

Tailgaters make me self-conscious because even though I know I'm going the proper speed, I hate the thought of the person stuck behind me cursing me out. I hate knowing that they are annoyed with me, even though they don't have a clue who I am.

I get nervous about other things too, like how I might run out of gas soon (even though the tank is still half full) and how a cop might be hiding behind the trees ready to pull me over (even though I've done nothing wrong).

I even worry about things as silly as the windshield wiper speed. Whenever the rain falls, I check if the other cars have their wipers set to move faster or slower than mine. To see if I'm being overly cautious or not cautious enough. I hate making quick decisions.

At yellow lights, it takes me a second to decide whether to keep going or to grind to a halt. I would rather have a red or a green. A way to avoid making choices so that I don't accidentally make the wrong one. I don't trust myself to do the right thing. I don't trust myself at all.

Even after I reach my destination, I get stressed out about parking – especially during a get-together or a house party. Do I pull into the person's driveway and risk blocking them inside when they might need to get out? Do I park in front of their neighbor's house and potentially piss them off? I overthink every little detail.

It gets worse if someone asks me to drive them home. While they are sitting in the passenger seat, I feel like I have to impress them. I feel pressure to drive perfectly, to merge perfectly, to park perfectly. I feel pressure to pick a song that they enjoy. I feel pressure to keep the temperature *just right* so they don't complain about being too hot or too cold.

If I make a mistake in front of them, I will try to laugh it off. I will hope they aren't judging me. That they aren't silently promising themselves that they will never accept a ride from me again.

By the time I drop them off, my cheeks are red with all the embarrassment and my hands are red from gripping the steering wheel tight enough to snap it in two.

20

Social Media Makes My Anxiety So Much Worse

Social media should make me feel more at ease since the interactions aren't happening face-to-face, forcing me to look the other person in the eyes, but it can be just as stressful. Whenever I get an unexpected notification, my heart races. If I receive an email from my boss or teacher or ex, it can take me a while to work up the energy to read it. I'll let it sit in my inbox until I conjure up the courage to hear what they have to say.

Before I send anything back or post on any form of social media – Instagram, Facebook, or Snapchat – I triple check what I wrote to make sure there aren't any spelling errors. I zoom in on the picture I'm about to post to make sure that there aren't any embarrassing zits on my face or messes in the background.

Even if I'm excited about sharing news about my new promotion or the vacation I took, I hesitate to tell the internet about it, worried that everyone will think that I am full of myself. That I am cocky. That I think I'm too good for them when really, the opposite is true.

After I go through with posting on any platform, I compulsively check to see how many likes I'm getting. If too much time goes by without enough outside approval, then I will freak out. I will feel like a complete idiot for posting at all, for assuming anyone else would care about what's going on in my life. Feeling like a failure, I will take the post down before anyone else sees so that no one notices how unpopular I am. How I don't even have enough friends to reach double-digit likes on a picture.

When it comes to other people's posts, I read too much into what they write. When they create vague statuses about how they are fed up with everyone and can't trust their friends, I hope I didn't upset them somehow. I hope they aren't indirectly talking about me, trying to give me a hint about how horrible I've been treating them, even though there's really no reason why their anger would have anything to do with me.

Sometimes, I even worry about tiny things, like whether I liked too many pictures in a row. I don't want someone to think I'm obsessed with them because I happened to see the last ten things they posted and pressed the heart button on every single one of them. I worry that my clicks are making me look pathetic, clingy, desperate.

Sometimes I wonder whether I should delete everything – my Instagram, my Facebook, my Tumblr, my Twitter. I wonder whether I would be better off without social media because it feels like it hurts me more than helps me. Like on the days when I'm too drained of energy to hold a conversation with friends, so I text them that I'm going to bed. Then I forget to stay off the grid, scroll through social media, and accidentally like their posts when I'm supposed to be asleep. It makes me look like a liar. It makes me seem like a bad friend.

It makes me *feel* like a bad friend.

21

Anxiety Makes It Hard To Talk Over The Phone

Making phone calls sends my nerves into a frenzy because I am paranoid that I am going to dial the wrong number. Even though the worst thing that could happen is the person on the other end of the line telling me I made a mistake, I still don't want to deal with that kind of embarrassment.

That's why I double (and triple) check the number a friend emailed me or the business number I found on Google, making sure that I punched in the right thing.

While the phone is ringing, a part of me is praying that they leave the call unanswered, so I can leave a voicemail instead. But then I worry about what would happen if it *did* go to voice-mail because if I said something awkward, they would be able to listen to the message again and again. It would act as a per-manent reminder of how antisocial I am.

Even though face-to-face conversations are intimidating, at least the other person can watch me nod my head along to whatever it is they're saying. When I'm speaking over the phone, I feel like I have to constantly make comments, because if I'm silent for too long, they will wonder where I went. They will wonder if I'm actually paying attention. They will feel like the conversation is one-sided.

Since I can never come up with anything clever to say on the spot, I will either fake a laugh or make an 'mhm' every five seconds to show them that I understand what they mean. Either that or I will say something generic like "that's so cool" or "that makes sense." Filler sentences with no depth behind them.

Not being able to see their body language freaks me out, because it's hard to determine exactly how they feel by the sound of their voice. Are they rolling their eyes at me? Are they smiling? Are they fidgeting like I am?

The entire time I'm on the phone, I pace around the room, too nervous to stay in one place. But I'm careful not to do anything that makes too much noise, like eat food or use the bathroom, because I don't want the other person to hear noises and wonder what the hell I am doing.

Even if they are the one who called me, even if they are the one leading the conversation, I still glance at the clock every few seconds. I worry about taking up too much of their time. I don't want to keep them on the hook for longer than they want to be there.

But I can never end a conversation smoothly. I don't know how to tell someone that the phone call is over, that I'm ready to hang up, without sounding rude. So I stay on the line for longer than I want to, even if I am swamped with work, even if I have other things to do. I try my best to look polite because I don't want to hurt anyone's feelings, even over the phone.

22

My Anxiety Comes Out Inside Of Restaurants

I hate meeting a group of people for dinner when I am driving there alone because I am always early. I always end up sitting in the parking lot for at least a half-hour, staring at my phone until the battery runs low, waiting for the rest of the group to show up so I can walk inside with someone else.

I know I should be brave and venture inside alone to give my name to the hostess, but even saying two or three sentences to a stranger makes my mouth run dry. Besides, the wait might not be as long as I think it will be. I might end up getting seated before anyone else arrives, and the tables around me will stare, wondering where the rest of my party is. Wondering why I am sitting there all by myself.

Unfortunately, when my friends finally arrive, when I am no longer alone, it doesn't necessarily mean that my anxiety is going to disappear.

I hate when my friends jump straight into detailed conversations about their lives without moving to pick up the menu. I hate having to send the waitress away for the third time because we still aren't ready to order. I hate feeling rude by staring at the paper in my hands instead of at the friend who is talking because I don't want to forget the name of the item I am ordering.

When the food finally arrives, I pray that the waitress brought me the right meal, because I would never dream of sending it back. After all, something as harmless as asking for ketchup sends me shaking. I know my friends wouldn't hesitate to get the job done for me, but I hate relying on them because it makes me appear childish.

None of them understand what my brain is putting me through. They don't understand how I hate eating in front of people because I worry that my lipstick is going to smudge or I'm going to get something caught in my teeth or I'm going to chew too loud. I'm worried that I will end up making them laugh at me instead of alongside me.

Of course, I would rather join my friends for dinner at a sit-down restaurant than at a bar. I hate having to walk up to the counter and push past a crowd of people to try to get the bartender's attention. I hate having my personal space invaded.

I also hate how loud those places can be, how it's impossible to hear what my friend – or some stranger who decided to approach me and strike up a conversation – is trying to scream over the speakers. I hate nodding like I agree with what they said, even though I never heard a word.

Most of all, I hate how often alcohol causes me to use the bathroom – because I hate *searching* for the bathroom. I have a fear that I'll walk the wrong way or shove through the wrong door or stumble into the kitchen. I have a fear I'll never find what I'm looking for, like in a dream when you walk and walk and walk but never gain any distance. That is what anxiety feels like. Like I am stuck in a bad dream.

23

I'm Worried Anxiety Will Ruin My Relationship

I feel guilty when I turn down certain date ideas because I am too terrified to go through with them. Because they involve crowds. Because they involve audience participation. Because they involve socializing with someone other than my boyfriend, the only person I feel comfortable beside.

At times, I feel like I am holding him back. Like I am standing in his way. Like I am stopping him from experiencing everything he deserves.

At times, I feel like he would be happier with someone else. Someone who would rather have fun with a big group on a Friday night instead of sitting at home. Someone who would be able to make new friends wherever she went instead of keeping quiet. Someone who would encourage him to step out of his comfort zone instead of spending her whole life afraid of leaving hers.

I know that everyone has issues and my boyfriend doesn't mind dealing with mine, that he is happy to stand by my side no matter how anxious I become, but I still feel bad.

I am always apologizing for something. *I'm sorry for being so quiet when we went out with your friends tonight, I know it looked rude. I'm sorry for canceling plans with you, I know you were excited about them. I'm sorry for ruining your day. I'm sorry for being a bad girlfriend. I'm sorry for being me.*

At least when I'm single, I feel like the only person my anxiety is hurting is myself. When I'm in a relationship, I feel like I'm hurting him, too.

Even though he tries his hardest to understand what I am going through, I can see how confused he gets when my anxiety comes out of the blue. He can wrap his mind around the reason why my heart beats fast and my voice goes shaky when I have an interview, a meeting, a speech, a ceremony. A milestone moment in my life.

But when we are going to hang out with his friends or visit his parents, I feel like I have to keep my symptoms to myself. I don't want him to get the wrong idea and assume I dislike the people who matter the most to him. That I am uncomfortable around them. That I don't want anything to do with them and would rather stay home.

The truth is that, yes, I would rather stay home on that particular day, but it's not because of the people we're going to see. It's because of the mindset I'm stuck in.

Sometimes I get anxious going to see friends I have known since high school, family members who helped raise me. The *person* doesn't matter. The idea of socializing does.

Even though my boyfriend has been understanding up until this point, I'm terrified of my anxiety figuring out a way to ruin our relationship, just like it has ruined everything else in my life. I'm terrified that it will eventually chase away the one person who has actually been able to handle my baggage.

24

Alcohol Makes Anxiety Easier To Deal With (For A Little While)

Around certain people, I feel more comfortable with a wine glass in my hand. With a beer balanced on the table in front of me. With vodka swishing through my stomach.

When I have alcohol inside of me, I have an easier time getting along with others. I can make jokes without wondering whether anyone will laugh. I can tell stories without worrying about how interesting they sound. I can be myself without the fear of being judged.

When I'm tipsy, I'm able to do the one thing that I have always wished I could do while sober. Socialize. I can stop wasting my time overanalyzing the way that someone looked at me or the tone they took with me. I finally feel comfortable. I feel at ease. I feel normal for once.

Even though it's unhealthy, I'm more inclined to stop by a party or join a group of friends at a restaurant if I know that alcohol is going to be served, because then I don't have to worry about how awkward I sound. I can drink until I stop caring what other people think.

Of course, I try to drink responsibly. I try not to go overboard. I try not to black out.

If I wake up the next morning without any memory of what happened, the questions kick in as early as the hangover. What did I do? What did I say? Did I dance in front of other people? Did I throw up in front of them? Did I reveal my secrets to them?

As much as I wish I could forget all of the awkward moments of my past, I hate not knowing whether or not I made an ass of myself the night before. I hate seeing friends the next day and wondering if they remember something that I can't recall. I hate paying even closer attention than usual to the way they stare at me and smile at me to see if they are treating me different. To see if there's any reason why I should worry.

That's why hungover-me will search through my phone for clues about what happened the previous night. I will check my photographs, I will check my social media, and I will check my texts. If I happen to find an embarrassing message written to an ex or a parent or even a close friend, then I will spend the rest of the day hating myself.

I will wish that I never picked up the bottle. I will promise myself the drinking needs to stop. I will try to accept that the alcohol might make me feel more relaxed in the moment, but that it makes things a million times worse the next day. It makes me even more paranoid than usual, and that's saying something.

I'm not some stupid kid. I know that relying on alcohol to socialize is dangerous. That I need to learn how to become comfortable with myself without the help of a well-stocked cooler. That I need to remember that people like me, even when I'm sober, even when I'm convinced they wish I would leave the room.

25

My Anxiety Makes Me Uncomfortable On Public Transportation

I would rather drive than step onto a bus or a train. But when I have no other choice except to take public transportation, I will do whatever I can to keep other people away from me. I will pop in my headphones so no one will try to talk to me. I will skim through a book to look like I'm too busy for a conversation. I will fold my arms, stare out the window, and look as unapproachable as possible.

Every time someone new steps onto the aisle, I will panic, hoping that they choose to sit somewhere else, anywhere else. I could leave my bag on the seat beside me to ward them off, but if the place is packed, I don't want to be rude. I don't want to leave someone stranded without a seat because my anxiety is acting up again.

If someone makes the mistake of choosing the seat beside me, I will avoid eye contact to prevent small talk. I will sit in the most uncomfortable position, just so there isn't any chance of bumping legs or shoulders with them. If they ask me a question, I will give them a one-word answer and if they comment on the weather or the drive, I will release a fake laugh. And throughout rest of the drive, that interaction is all I will think about – how I can't even hold a two-second conversation without embarrassing myself.

Of course, sitting next to a complete stranger (even a talkative one) beats being forced to stand on the bus. When that happens, I worry about whether it is going to come to a sudden stop and I am going to stumble into the person in front of me. I worry about whether the bag on my arm is going to smack into the person sitting beside me by accident. I worry about whether the people standing behind me are staring at my ass or whether the person sitting eye-level with my crotch is looking that way.

When I'm not distracted by my slew of people problems, I worry about getting onto the wrong bus or train. Missing my stop. Ending up somewhere miles away from my intended destination. I worry that I made a stupid mistake that will screw up my schedule (even though I triple checked the times before leaving the house and looked again at the station).

Even if I'm positive I took the correct bus, I worry about the driver. I worry that they are going too fast, fast enough to cause an accident – or that they are moving too slow, slow enough to make me late for my appointment.

If I am running behind, I will check my phone again and again for the time, as if seeing those numbers will change anything. Of course, even if I am making good time, worst case scenarios still pop into my thoughts. What if the bus breaks down? What if the train derails? What if the driver skips my stop for some reason?

What if everything that can go wrong *does* go wrong?

26

I Get Anxiety Every Time I Visit The Hair Salon

I hate trips to the hair salon, starting from the moment I have to call up and schedule an appointment. Even though I usually avoid phones at all costs, I would never walk into a salon spontaneously and risk the owner telling me that they are filled up for the day, that I should come back some other time. I can't handle rejection, even on such a small scale.

Even after booking an appointment, when I walk through the salon doors, I worry that my name isn't going to be written down for some reason. I worry that they will turn me away, even though I planned ahead. Then I take things further and worry that they will refuse to do what I ask them to do. That they will tell me dying my hair *that* color will destroy it or will look weird with my skin tone.

I have a fear the workers are going to sit me down, run their hands through my hair, and point out all of its flaws. *It is too dry. It is too thin. There are too many dead ends.* I don't want a professional to pick apart my appearance when I do the same thing every morning as I stare into the mirror.

Some people find the salon relaxing, but I am uncomfortable

the entire time. I feel weird sitting in silence, staring blankly at my reflection or down at the cape covering my lap, while everyone else is chatting to their stylist. The worst part is that they aren't even engaging in small talk. No. They are talking about deep parts of their life. They are going into detail about their kids and college and surgeries. They are telling their life stories with ease.

Meanwhile, when my hair dresser asks me a question, I give her a short answer. An answer that ends the conversation before it begins. An answer that makes it look like I want to be left alone, like I don't want to talk – which is the truth, but I hate how snobby it makes me seem.

To overcompensate for my silence, I will drown her in compliments when my haircut is finished. It doesn't matter if I secretly hate the length or the style. Instead of telling her I would like it changed, to remind her I am paying her to do what makes *me* happy, I will lie about how amazing it looks. I will compliment her, leave a nice tip, and fake a smile until I reach my car and cry my eyes out over how horrible it looks.

But it will never cross my mind to confront the woman. To walk back into the salon and get the style fixed, free of charge, which she would probably be happy to take care of for me. Instead, I will either deal with it until it grows out again – or if it's *really* bad, I will go to another salon, waste another hundred dollars, to get what I would have gotten in the first place if I was brave enough to speak my mind.

27

Anxiety Makes Me Look Like An Asshole

I don't reach out to people.

I'm terrified of talking on the phone and starting conversations with strangers. I'm even scared of texting certain friends and coming on too strong, of graduating from a concerned friend to an annoying nuisance. So I delete messages. I wait too long to answer back. I don't let on that I care.

But I care more than anyone realizes. I care so much it hurts.

I come across as a snob because I find it hard to talk, hard to force a smile. But I'm not trying to be a bitch. I'm only trying to survive — because, to me, social interaction is a war zone. It makes my cheeks redden, my lungs flutter.

That's why I don't look people in the eye as they're talking to me. I look at their lipstick, at the wall behind them, I might even glance down at my phone. It makes me seem like I don't give a damn about what they have to say, but avoiding their gaze is just a crutch. I'm paying closer attention than they can imagine. Absorbing every word.

I'm not a good conversationalist — and it makes me seem like a shitty friend.

I don't jump into conversations. I'm quiet in groups. People assume that I'm sitting there, judging them for every word that pops out of their lips when really I'm in awe of how easily they can communicate. How natural it is for them. How human they are and how fucked up I am.

Of course, they don't realize that I have anxiety. They just think I'm quiet. Shy.

No, they don't realize I have anxiety because I'm not shaking at the table and hyperventilating into a paper bag. My meltdowns happen *before* I see them.

The night before, on my drive there, in the car — I'm freaking out the entire time. Imagining all of the things that could go wrong. Picturing how embarrassed I'll be.

But when I'm finally in public, I internalize everything. I try to minimize my physical symptoms to avoid drawing attention to myself — but just because I calmed my shaking doesn't mean I've calmed my mind.

I'm still anxious. I'm just not showing it. Secretly, I'm freaking out over what I look like. Freaking out over what to say next. Freaking out over why someone across the room gave me a strange look.

And if I need to compose myself, I'll escape to the bathroom and heavy breathe inside of a stall or splash water across my face, and then walk back into the room like I'm perfectly fine.

But I'm not fine. Anxiety makes sure I'm *never* fine.

It makes me hate myself. It makes me turn down opportunities that I know I'd enjoy. It makes me stay quiet when I have something important to say.

It makes me look like a complete asshole.

But that's not true at all. I'm just someone that's trying to get through the day. Someone that wants to be liked but feels like they'll never belong.

28

My Anxiety Puts Me Through Stress While Shopping

Anxiety can transform the most basic chores into the most terrifying experiences.

Whenever I go to the grocery store on a search for something specific, I make a promise to find it on my own. It doesn't matter if I have been scanning the aisles for ten minutes straight and still can't find what I'm looking to purchase. I will continue to walk in circles instead of getting a worker's attention and asking for help. I will do anything within my power to avoid speaking to another human being.

I don't even like being in the vicinity of other people. If I need to grab food from an aisle that is packed with people, I will find the next thing on my list and return when the crowd disperses. I don't want to deal with them for a second, even if it's only to ask them to move their cart so I can grab the cereal I want.

That's the reason why I use the self-checkout whenever I have the chance. I hate making small talk with the cashier. I hate the possibility of my debit card getting declined, even though I just checked the account and know that there is more than enough money inside.

Most of all, I hate when I pay in cash and the transaction ends. I hate receiving change back and having to stuff it back in my wallet as quickly as possible so that the people queued behind me don't get frustrated and huff about how I'm holding up the line.

It is even worse when I go to a clothing store littered with workers whose job it is to stroll over to me as soon as I enter. I know they have to talk to me, so I don't want to appear rude, but listening to their sales pitches makes me feel uncomfortable. I never know how to tell them I'm not interested without looking like another asshole customer.

I try my best to avoid stores like that, especially when the workers stare at me as I'm browsing through their selection. Even though I'm not doing anything wrong, I hate the feeling of being watched. I hate knowing that someone else's eyes are glued to me. It makes my cheeks flush red and my mouth run dry.

Dressing rooms make me just as nervous because I'm always worried that I'm taking up too much time. That someone is outside waiting, whether it's another customer who wants to use the room or a worker who wants to take their lunch break as soon as I'm finished.

When I finally am finished, I feel weird placing too many things back on the hook and walking out without making a purchase. I'm worried about looking like I swiped something to jam inside my bag. I'm worried about setting off the alarms on the door, even though there is nothing to find.

Because of my anxiety, I do most of my shopping online where there is no one around to judge me. I might end up with the wrong sized jeans. I might pay more than I should for shipping. But at least I won't end up hyperventilating in my car afterward.

29

My Anxiety Doesn't Go Away While I'm Asleep

My anxiety follows me into my sleep.

Instead of having sweet dreams about kissing my person or meeting my favorite celebrity – or even nightmares about monsters chasing me through forests and swallowing me whole – I have realistic dreams. Dreams that feel all too real.

I have dreams about showing up late to class and getting punished by the professor. About forgetting to prepare for a big test and being unable to answer one question correctly. About embarrassing myself in front of a group of teenagers that are now grown adults, because I graduated years ago.

I have dreams about sliding past stop signs and into traffic because my brakes stopped working. About swerving off the road because I jerked the wheel the wrong way on accident. About losing control of my car the same way that I have lost control of my life.

I have dreams about getting lost on my way to work on the day of an important meeting. About getting fired from my job for screwing up one too many times. About losing everything that I worked so hard to achieve because I don't know how to hold onto happiness.

I have dreams about my person cheating on me with someone younger, prettier. About finding out they never liked me in the first place and only dated me as a joke. About realizing that I am alone once again and this is the way it is meant to be, this is the fate I deserve.

I have dreams about standing in front of my closet and struggling to find the right outfit for the day. About walking winding halls and not being able to find a bathroom in a public place. About the most boring, mundane things that a person could possibly dream about. My worries during daylight carry over to my unconscious when the sun sets.

My dreams have hurt me so badly that I have been nudged awake in the middle of the night because I was crying. I have sobbed while fast asleep without even realizing what was happening. I have woken up with damp pillowcases and dark thoughts.

The worst part is that once I'm fully awake, the dream continues to haunt me, because it didn't contain monsters I can laugh about now that I'm in my right mind. It contained problems that could actually happen in real life. It contained my deepest fears.

On the mornings I can remember my dreams, I wish I could erase them from my mind to ease my paranoia. Even though I know the dream isn't a reflection of reality, for the rest of the day I will be extra worried about my job or my relationship or my driving.

On the other hand, if I have no memory of the dream after my lids flutter open, the uncomfortable feeling remains – and that can be just as stressful. It raises too many questions. What could have possibly made me that upset? A dream about my friends abandoning me? Or my cat dying? Or my grandmother getting sick? I'll spend the whole day trying to jog my memory because my anxiety refuses to give me a moment of rest.

30

Anxiety Makes Me Feel Like A Horrible Girlfriend

I feel like a shitty girlfriend every time I make an excuse for how I'm not really in the mood to go out tonight. Every time I follow my boyfriend around at a party because I'm terrified of being stuck in a conversation with friends of friends. Every time I get quiet around his parents, even though I should be comfortable around them by now.

I hate how long it takes me to get used to a new situation. I don't want to be the girl who seems like she's stuck up, quiet, a bitch.

I want to be the girl who hugs his mother hello, who makes jokes that his father laughs at, who doesn't need alcohol in her system in order to spend the night with a group of his closest friends — who should also be my closest friends since we see each other so often.

I feel like a shitty girlfriend because my anxiety stops me from acting carefree and fun.

Even when we're alone together, there are times when my anxiety gets the best of me. Even though I'm more comfortable around him than anyone else I've ever met. Even though I trust him. Even though I don't mind when he sees me scared and vulnerable.

But still, I can't help myself from feeling insecure.

I feel like a shitty girlfriend because I start fights over stupid things. I get mad about the way he looked at me or spoke to me. And I get quiet when we have a waitress who can talk with ease, who can instantly make anyone like her — because she's the type of girl I wish I was and imagine he wishes he was with.

My anxiety makes me feel like a shitty girlfriend because I know he wants me to admit when something is bothering me, but I still pretend I'm fine. I lie to him to make things easier on myself.

I'm so used to hiding my feelings, I'm used to acting like I'm okay when I'm not at all. It's hard to get used to opening up to someone. It's weird to know that someone likes me for me, even when I'm having irrational thoughts that would make anyone else in my life uncomfortable.

My anxiety makes me feel like a shitty girlfriend because I ruin dates by overthinking. I worry about whether we're going to get somewhere on time or follow the right directions. I worry about everything there is to worry about. I can never enjoy a good thing, even when I'm sitting beside the love of my life.

My anxiety makes me feel like a shitty girlfriend because that's what anxiety does. It makes me doubt myself. It makes me hate myself.

My anxiety makes me feel like a shitty girlfriend — even though my boyfriend keeps reminding me that it's not the case. That he's lucky to have me. That he wants to be with me forever, whether I'm suffering from anxiety or not.

31

Because Of My Anxiety, I Am Always Uncomfortable

I never feel relaxed. I never feel safe. I am always on the edge of my seat, worrying about what will happen next. I am always waiting for whatever ounce of happiness that I have to be yanked away from me. For the charade of calmness to come to an end.

I am scared to send the first text because if the person takes too long to answer me, I will feel like our entire friendship is a lie, like no one wants me around. I am scared to speak to strangers in shops and street corners because I am worried about being judged, I am worried that they will see exactly who I am and realize it isn't anyone good.

I am scared to raise my hand in class. Scared to send emails to my bosses. Scared to dance at parties. Scared to leave my house to socialize. Scared to exist.

And I am scared of bigger things. I am scared of death. I am scared of walking through darkened city streets and riding packed subway cars and merging onto busy highways because of the horror splattered across news tickers. Because I am worried about becoming another statistic.

I am even scared when I am inside of my own home. When I am around the people who are supposed to make me feel at ease, like there is nothing to worry about. I can't trust anyone. I can only trust myself.

But at the same time, I can't even trust myself. I can't trust my memories because I will replay a conversation in my mind again and again until I realize that the other person looked at me wrong, that they spoke sarcastically, that they seemed annoyed.

When that doubt creeps inside, I don't know whether I am being a realist or being ridiculous. Whether I am overreacting or finally seeing things the way they were meant to be seen.

Fear follows me everywhere and my insecurities tag alone, too.

I am always uncomfortable, no matter the situation. During long silences, I freak out, hoping the other person isn't bored with me. And when they are speaking, instead of fully paying attention to their words, I pay attention to whether I'm making too much eye contact with them or not enough. Either that or I fumble through my brain, trying to come up with the response I am going to give them once they stop talking.

I am only half listening. I am only half there. I am only half existing at any given time.

I am always uncomfortable, even when I am alone because that is when I have the most time to think. And thinking is the worst thing for me. My brain is my worst enemy. It convinces me that I am unattractive. Unlovable. Unbearable. It makes me doubt whether I deserve all of the good things in my life — and convinces me I deserve all the bad things.

I am always uncomfortable. It has always been that way and I am worried that is never going to change.

32

I Always Feel Anxious Inside Of Movie Theaters

Even a lighthearted trip to the movies with friends can trigger my anxiety.

I hate the idea of arriving anywhere late, even if that means I'm going to have to sit through twenty minutes of previews before the movie starts. The idea of walking into a crowded theater overflowing with people who have already taken their seats and settled in for the film makes me feel uncomfortable, like I am being disrespectful somehow

Of course, showing up early can be even worse, because my friends might ask me to save their seats for them while they venture over to the concession stand. Resting my jacket on one or two chairs is fine, but there is nothing more uncomfortable than trying to reserve an entire row. I'm worried someone will complain about how *if my friends really wanted those seats, they would be sitting in them.*

I hate confrontation, no matter how small it may be. That is why, whenever I am given the option, I choose the aisle seat. I want an easy escape in case something goes wrong. I don't want to be blocked in by strangers, suffocated by their body heat, so I keep my distance whenever possible.

Of course, when the theater is packed and it is impossible to remain inside my personal bubble, I do whatever I can to avoid drawing attention to myself. If I have to go to the bathroom, I will hold it for as long as possible, so I don't have to scoot past strangers and block the screen. If I buy food, I try to buy something soft, a snack that won't make much noise when my teeth crack down on it.

I will get anxious about the dumbest things. Whether the sound of my laugh is obnoxious, whether it is the kind of laugh that other people flinch when hearing because it is *that* annoying. Whether I am coughing too loud or readjusting my position too often and the people around me are wishing that I would keep my mouth closed and my body still.

Sometimes, I even ruin my friends' fun, because I refuse to whisper-scream my comments in an overcrowded room. I can wait until afterward, when we grab dinner, to tell them my thoughts on the film. Inside of the silent theater – where people paid over ten bucks per ticket – I prefer to stay quiet, to act respectfully.

It bothers me when my friends talk too loud. When they make jokes that the row in front of us can hear. When they use their cellphone and everyone behind them can see the flash of light. Even though I'm not the one causing the distraction, I'm associated with them and that is enough to put me on edge. To make me worry whether someone is going to approach us, grab us by the arm, and kick us out.

I hate how it's a struggle for me to enjoy something that is meant to be fun. I hate that I find problems everywhere I look.

33

I Always Get Anxious About My Health

Whenever I hear sirens from an ambulance whooshing down the street, I worry that someone I love is hurt. Even though the chances are low that one of my family members or friends are in trouble, I can't shake the feeling of fear until I hear from them again.

Of course, I don't want to sound crazy by texting them and asking if they are still alive, so I send a casual message asking them if they saw a certain show last night or if they are having a good week. The longer they take to respond, the more I start to sweat, but they never know it. I keep that secret to myself.

However, when I'm the one who isn't feeling well, I avoid the doctor at all costs. The idea of picking up the phone and making an appointment is too nerve-racking, not to mention the fact that I would have to take off a full day from work in order to make it down to the doctor's office.

I hate when sickness ruins my routine. I don't want to miss class and have a pile of work to return to when I get better. I don't want to cancel plans with my friends and risk them hating my guts. I don't want to spend time sleeping when I should be getting important work done.

Instead of consulting a professional, I check my symptoms online and create a self-diagnosis, which leads down a rabbit hole. I know that chances are, I only have a cold. However, when some of my symptoms suggest that I could have diabetes or AIDS or cancer, I end up caving and going to the doctor anyway. Just to be safe.

I try to dress my best when I feel my worst because even though I'm going to be surrounded by other red-eyed patients, I don't want to look like a mess. I don't want to leave the house without looking decent. I don't want the doctor or nurse or worker behind the front desk to judge me.

When I reach the office and take a seat, I feel uneasy the entire time. I hate getting seated beside patients who are sicker than I am, who could pass on their germs to me. I hate the thought that sitting in the waiting room could make me worse instead of better. I hate wondering whether I'm wasting my time because the cold would go away on its own, or whether I'm going to be redirected to the hospital because the diagnosis is worse than I imagined.

And I hate waiting for the nurse to call my name because I'm worried that I won't hear their voice over the voices in my own head (or that I will mishear them, assume they called me, and get up during the wrong moment, making a fool out of myself). Even when I should only be thinking about my health, I'm still thinking about the way I look to others. I'm still hoping that no one judges me.

34

Anxiety Ruins My Conversations On Dating Apps

Whenever I go through a long stretch of being single, I blame my fear of engaging with new people, of putting myself out there, of actually stepping foot outside of my house. I consider my anxiety responsible for my loneliness.

I download dating apps because, in theory, it should be considerably less stressful than dressing up, going to the bar, and chatting up strangers. Swiping right is easier than making eye contact from across a crowded room, but when it comes time to actually talk, my nerves reveal themselves.

I never send the first message, because just like in real life, I never know what to say. It doesn't matter that they swiped right for me too, proving they want to get to know me better. In my mind, they might have done that for everyone. Their finger might have slipped. Or they might have swiped me as a joke.

Even after having a few successful conversations, I avoid checking my dating apps, afraid of what I will find. I will be upset if the person I thought I had a real chance with failed to answer my last message because that must mean they aren't interested. It must mean they found someone better.

But at the same time that I'm praying they answered me, I'm also worried about the potential things that they could have said. What if they want to take things a step further? What if they ask to see me in person? What if they ask me on an actual, official date?

Nine out of ten times, I end up turning someone down – not because of lack of interest in them, but because the thought of meeting them makes me hyperventilate.

What if they are disappointed because I looked better in my profile pictures? What if things get awkward when there is a lull in conversation? What if they realize spending time with me was a mistake?

Even worse, what if they expect me to pick the dating spot? I hate when other people ask for me to choose a time and a place because I would rather sit back and let them make the decision. That way, at least I would know they are happy with the plans. If I'm the one choosing, then there is a chance that I will make a mistake. That I will ruin the date before it even begins.

There is too much stress when it comes to relationships, which is why I tend to cancel dates at the last second. As much as my heart is pushing me to go, my head convinces me to stay home instead.

Of course, I am too ashamed to tell the truth about the situation, so the other person never understands the real reason why I am backing out and assumes that I am fickle. Flaky. Unreliable. Rude.

After being hurt by me once, they never want to stick around and risk having me do the same thing a second time – and I can't blame them. I wouldn't want to date myself either.

35

Everyone With Anxiety Is Trying Their Best

I might not hold a conversation well, but I will listen to everything that you say. I won't stare at my phone while you are talking. I won't daydream about what I am going to be doing later. I will absorb every word that comes out of your mouth. I will give you the attention that you deserve. I will remember the date of your birthday and the time of your classes. I will memorize the names of your cousins and coworkers. I will retain whatever you say to me because I really do care, even if it looks like I am not paying any attention.

I might not send out the first text or invite you over to my house, but I will always be thinking of you. I will think of you when your favorite song comes on the radio. When I see a shirt at the mall that I could imagine you wearing. When I see a dog or a cat who looks like the one you have. I might not reach out to tell you any of those things because I don't want you to think of me as clingy. I don't want to come on too strong. I don't want to seem awkward because the last thing I want is for you to cut me out of your life. The last thing I want is for you to think I'm weird and walk away.

I might not be the life of the party, but I will come along if you want me there. If going someplace is important to you, then I will fight against my anxiety and abandon my comfort zone. I might not talk to anyone. I might sit in the corner by myself the entire time. I might hide in the bathroom to escape all the noise. But I will be nice to anyone who walks over to me. I will smile at them if they smile at me. I will try my best to be friendly.

I might not tell you how much you mean to me, but I will show you in as many different ways as I can. By spending weeks picking out the perfect birthday present for you. By having your favorite foods stocked in my fridge in case you come over. By offering to pay for your drinks when we go out to eat together. By going out of my way to do things for you that I only do for people who truly matter to me.

I might not be the best friend or daughter or sister or girlfriend in the world — I might go missing for a few days when my anxiety acts up or tell you that I'm fine when I am secretly dying inside because I don't want to bother you with my pain — but I will always try my hardest to make you happy. I will try my hardest to be there for you in the same way you have always been there for me.

36

Since My Anxiety Stops Me From Getting Close To People, You Have No Idea What You Mean To Me

My anxiety stops me from texting other people first and asking them to hang out and using too many emojis. It stops me from showing my excitement and convinces me to act emotionless so I don't embarrass myself.

My anxiety makes me seem like I don't care about the people who mean the most to me — and I hate the thought of those people not realizing how much I love them. How I would do anything for them.

There were so many times when I wanted to text you but didn't want to be a bother. There were so many times when I wanted to remind you how much I love you but didn't want to come on too strong. There are so many things I have always wanted to say to you but never found the strength.

That's why I want to take the time to tell you how much I care about you. How much I appreciate all of the times that you've texted me and asked to hang out, even if I told you I was too busy to meet up. I appreciate all of the times you have reached out to me, whether it was to ask me a question or wish me a happy birthday.

You have no idea how much those little things mean to me. How long I hold onto the happiness that a text from your phone or a smile from your face brings me.

I want to thank you for being there for me through it all. During my good and bad days. I want to thank you for spending time with me, even when I was silent throughout an entire conversation and made things awkward. Even when it would have been easier for you to walk away than deal with me.

I'm sorry that my anxiety makes it difficult to make plans with me. I'm sorry that my anxiety stops me from being as open with you as I wish I could be. I'm sorry that my anxiety has put up this invisible barrier between us. I really am.

I'm sorry that my anxiety stops me from seeing you as much as I would like, that it stops me from getting as close to you as I wish I could get — but I never want you to feel like I don't care. I never want you to hear my nervous laughter and one-word answers and assume that means that I don't like you — because that's far from the truth.

You mean the world to me. I might not talk to you as often as I should, but I talk *about* you all the time. You're such a huge part of my life.

I think about you every single day. Even though I might not invite you over to my place or text you just because, you're always in the back of my mind.

Since I'm so bad at showing it, I want to take the time to tell you how much I love you. And how I couldn't imagine living this life without you.

I'm sorry that it's taken me so long to let you know that.

37

Never Date A Girl With Anxiety

Never date a girl with anxiety unless you are willing to give her the reassurance that she craves. Reassurance that she isn't being a bother. That she isn't talking too much. That she isn't texting back too fast. That she isn't being as annoying as she thinks. You need to give her reassurance that you still like her. That you haven't gotten bored of her. That you would never dream of cheating on her. That she is the only person for you.

Never date a girl with anxiety unless you are comfortable with silence. Because there are some days when she won't feeling like saying a word. When she will just want to cuddle with you in the quiet. There are going to be some days when she won't want to talk about what's bothering her. In fact, there will be some days when she won't even be able to put her finger on what's bothering her because nothing specific triggered her anxiety. It just appeared out of nowhere.

Never date a girl with anxiety unless you are okay with the fact that shit happens. Sometimes, she would rather stay home than leave the house for a date. Sometimes, she would rather stay in bed than get dressed. When that happens, she doesn't want you to look at her with disappointment. She doesn't need you to make her feel like a screw-up. She already feels that way most of the time.

Never date a girl with anxiety unless you understand that it is not her fault. She can't control the obsessive thoughts that pop into her head. She doesn't *want* her hands or her voice to shake. She doesn't want to hide inside of bathrooms and cancel plans at the last second. But she can't help it.

Never date a girl with anxiety unless you are willing to put effort into the relationship. If you take too long to answer her texts or act distant even though you're sitting face-to-face, then she is going to overthink. She is going to assume that you aren't happy with her. She is going to drown in her insecurities.

Never date a girl with anxiety unless you are willing to make plans ahead of time. She won't be happy if you spring something on her. If you tell her that she's having dinner with your parents or going to a friend's house party at the last second. She isn't a fan of surprises because she likes to plan ahead. She likes to have the chance to mentally prepare herself for socializing.

Never date a girl with anxiety unless you *really* like her. Unless you mean it when you tell her that her anxiety isn't a deal breaker. Unless you can look her directly in the eyes and promise her that you aren't going anywhere.

Never date a girl with anxiety unless you are going to treat her right. Unless you are willing to love her with all your heart on her good days *and* on her bad days.

38

My Anxiety Mixes Together With My OCD

Back when I was younger, when my OCD was at its worst, I used to flick the light switch on and off. On and off. On and off. I used to rise from my couch, sit back down, rise, and sit until I felt like I did it correctly. I used to avoid stepping on certain floor tiles. I used to repeat words under my breath.

I used to feel like a crazy person like I belonged inside of an institution.

Since then, I have learned to manage the most extreme symptoms of my OCD, but sometimes the urges return in subtle ways. Sometimes I will be reading a book, stumble over a word inside my head, and force myself to reread the same paragraph over and over again until I no longer make a mistake. Other times, I will force myself to read another chapter when my eyes are threatening to close when all I want to do is head to bed because I need to end on an even chapter instead of an odd one.

Sometimes, when I'm rushing to get ready in the morning, I tell myself that I can't wear the shirt I want to wear because it is bad luck (but only today, tomorrow it will be fine again).

Sometimes, when I'm listening to music in my car, I skip my favorite song because the song is bad luck. Sometimes, I won't eat what I want to eat, because the food is bad luck. Bad luck, bad luck, bad luck.

There is no reason for me to think that. There is no correlation that makes any semblance of sense. My brain makes up the rules and then forces me to obey – or there will be consequences. Some of the consequences are silly, like if you wear a purple shirt today, then you are going to be late to class. Some of the consequences are more extreme, like if you don't read one more chapter tonight then your father will die in a car crash.

OCD comes with self-awareness. I know how crazy my thoughts sound, I know that realistically nothing is going to happen if I wear purple or shut my book, but another part of my brain warns me to listen to those insane thoughts. Just in case.

I give into the compulsions because it eases my anxiety. I give into the compulsions because it quiets the needling thoughts in my head. At least for a little while.

Of course, there are always more OCD thoughts right around the corner. Before I fall asleep, I will have to position my pillow a certain way and say specific prayers – not because it brings me comfort, because it feels right. I always have to do what feels right, what my brain tells me will lower the risk of having some unspeakable horror happen to the people I love.

Unfortunately, my OCD makes my anxiety worse and my anxiety makes my OCD worse. It's a never-ending cycle that pushes me closer and closer to insanity.

39

I'm Worried Anxiety Will Make Me Lose My Job

My closest friends and family members are aware of my battle with anxiety. I try my best to avoid breaking down in front of them, but if it happens, it isn't the end of the world. However, the last thing I want to do is embarrass myself in the workplace. I don't want my peers to see me as someone to pity, someone who doesn't have their act together, someone who doesn't deserve their position.

Anxiety sucks the most when I'm stuck in the office because I can say no to my friends, to my parents, or to my romantic partners, but I can never say no to my boss. It would be career suicide. It would make me look like a lazy worker. Like the opposite of a team player.

If my boss wants to talk to me one-on-one, there is no way I can get out of the interaction. If my boss wants me to make a phone call, I have to suck it up and deal with it. If my boss wants me to give a presentation, I have to go through with it donning a smile.

At work, I can't use my anxiety as an excuse to get out of doing things that I am uncomfortable doing. If I cannot perform my job properly, then I am going to lose my job. It's as simple as that.

Of course, the anxiety doesn't end when my boss leaves the room. It is just as bad with my coworkers. I am not the kind of person who will strike up a conversation about what I did last weekend over the water cooler. I am not the kind of person who will invite everyone over to my place to watch the game.

My anxiety stops me from getting close to the people that I deal with every single day. Even though we spend five times a week together, we barely know each other. And since I feel like they are coworkers instead of friends, I turn down all of their invitations out.

Even if I secretly want to get drinks with the rest of them, I will feel weird agreeing to meet them at the bar. Who am I going to sit next to? What am I going to talk to them about? What if no one actually wants me there? What if they only invited me to be polite? What if they only invited me because they assumed I would turn them down as usual?

I feel weird participating in group conversations and attending holiday parties because I feel like I'm an outsider. Like I'm not aware of the inside jokes that everyone else laughs about while I'm eating lunch by myself. Like everyone else is part of this big, happy family while I am excluded.

And that is my own fault. My anxiety convinces me to keep my distance. It tells me to separate my social life from my work life because my coworkers would probably prefer it that way.

40

Anxiety Makes Me Jump To Crazy Conclusions

My anxiety forces me to jump to conclusions. Conclusions that can ruin my friendships, my relationships, my career, my entire life.

When someone takes too long to answer a simple text, I assume that they hate me. That they want nothing to do with me. Even though that's probably far from the truth, I convince myself that they would have answered by now if they actually cared.

When they finally text back, I should laugh off my paranoia and accept the fact that they aren't going anywhere. But for some reason, I hold onto my earlier conclusion. The idea that they hate me stays stuck in my head. I can't remove it, no matter how hard I try.

It creates a dangerous chain reaction. I will avoid sending the first text in the future because I don't want to bother them – but from their side of the fence, it looks like I don't care about them. It makes me seem like a bad friend. I will end up ruining a friendship by trying to avoid ruining the friendship.

The same thing happens with dating. Even if someone has

given me a million signals that show they are interested, I will freak out when I see them post a picture with another girl. Instead of talking to them, instead of actually asking who the mystery girl is, I assume that it must be his real love interest. The girl that he wants to date. The girl that he wants to marry.

I never consider the possibility that she could be a sister, a best friend, a cousin. I jump to the worst case scenario because I expect to be disappointed. I expect to have my heart broken. I expect to be replaced by someone better.

My anxiety convinces me that I am unlovable, which is why I see the world through such a negative lens. I assume that my boss hates me because he never interacts with me, instead of assuming that I must be doing such a good job that I don't need supervision. I assume that strangers are laughing at me anytime I catch them smiling, instead of assuming that they are laughing at something on their phone.

I assume that everyone sees me as a failure because that is the way I see myself. I assume the lies that my anxiety tells me, about being unattractive and annoying, are all true.

That is why I jump to conclusions every time a friend cancels plans with me at the last second. Every time my boss asks to speak with me one-on-one in his office. Every time that my crush glances at another girl who is prettier than me.

I assume that everyone secretly hates me, so whenever someone hurts me, I take it as proof that I was right. That I am a waste of space.

My anxiety makes me overthink every little thing that happens throughout my day. It makes me jump to conclusions that are completely ridiculous to everyone else – but feel all too real to me.

41

The Kind Of Person You Should Date When You Suffer From Anxiety

Date someone who understands that they are not always going to understand what you are going through. Someone who can accept the fact that your brain works differently than theirs does instead of constantly questioning you about what caused you to feel the way you are feeling. Someone who knows that you can't always explain what triggered you.

Date someone who is able to calm you down when all you want to do is collapse. Someone who will hold you close and squeeze when you want to feel them against you – but will give you a few minutes of solitude when you would rather crawl into bed and be left alone. Someone who understands that sometimes the best thing they can do is cradle you in silence and sometimes the best thing they can do is leave the room.

Date someone who doesn't get frustrated with you over the things that you have no control over. Someone who doesn't feel like you are inconveniencing them when you ask to sit in the car for a few minutes before walking inside of a restaurant.

Someone who doesn't accuse you of being unfriendly when you don't say a word to their friends all night long.

Date someone who takes your anxiety into consideration before making plans. Someone who checks with you before promising their parents that you will come to a holiday dinner. Someone who asks if you would be comfortable going to a certain concert before buying the tickets. Someone who tries their best to make you feel safe.

Date someone who reassures you when your anxiety takes control of you. Someone who reminds you that you are intelligent enough and strong enough to achieve any goals that you set. Someone who motivates you to at least try your hand at that thing you've been daydreaming about because you are going to do better than you believe. Someone who helps you venture outside of your comfort zone, but never pushes you out of that comfort zone if you really aren't ready.

Date someone who will give you the reassurance that you need without getting offended by you doubting them. Someone who won't look at you weird when you ask them to confirm whether or not you've been annoying lately. Someone who understands that you will occasionally need them to remind you that they love you, that they care about you, and that they aren't going to leave you. Someone who is happy to give you as much affection as you need, because they want you to feel loved.

Date someone who will listen to your anxious thoughts without calling you crazy. Without making you feel like you are being judged. Someone who will sit there and let you talk for as long as you need to talk. Someone who makes you feel like you aren't as flawed as you always thought.

Date someone who is patient with you. Understanding of

you. Someone who doesn't let your anxiety get in the way of loving you.

42

My Anxiety Makes Me Feel Like A Failure

I feel like a failure because even when I'm happy, I am unable to enjoy the moment. I'm always thinking about what could go wrong. About how things *never* go well for me, so if life has been going smoothly lately, something horrible must be lurking around the corner.

I feel like a failure because I'm terrified of things that an 'average' person would never think twice about. Getting stuck sitting next to a stranger on the bus. Stepping into a crowded elevator. Eating alone in the break room.

I feel like a failure because my miniature mistakes feel massive. Someone else might blush and laugh off an awkward moment, but I will think about it for days. Weeks. Years. I'll never stop replaying those embarrassing moments in my head.

I feel like a failure because my best is never good enough. Even if I try my hardest, I can still come up with a list of mistakes I made, with a reason why I could have done better. I will always hate myself for not doing more, for not reaching my full potential.

I feel like a failure because I dwell on what went wrong for longer than I should. My mistakes occupy all of my time, all of my thoughts. They torture me. They become the only thing I can think about during late nights when sleep refuses to come to me.

I feel like a failure because everyone else makes life look so easy. They can get up on stage and give a speech when I can barely look a friend in the eye during a conversation. When I can barely introduce myself without stumbling over the words.

I feel like a failure because the worst case scenario is the only one I pay any attention to. I never think about the good things that could happen to me. I only think about all the ways I could embarrass myself, all the ways I could ruin my life.

I feel like a failure because I can't stop myself from comparing my personality to everyone around me. I'm not as talkative as other people. I'm not as friendly as them. Not as interesting as them. I feel like I have nothing to offer.

I feel like a failure because I'm full of self-doubt. I feel like I don't fit in and never will. I feel like everyone deserves happiness, except for me.

I feel like a failure because no one congratulates me on the little things, the things that are actually the hardest for me to bring myself to do. Making a phone call. Ordering food. Going on a first date. Attending a party.

I feel like a failure because it's easy to forget that my little successes are still successes — that every time I talk to a stranger or ask a question in class, I should be proud of myself. I should feel a little less like a failure.

43

My Anxiety Keeps Getting In The Way

My anxiety stops me from getting close to people. I turn down invitations out. I end conversations early. I have trouble making eye contact and smiling and accepting compliments. I put up an invisible barrier between myself and the rest of the world. I push people away by accident.

My anxiety stops me from being productive. I spend too long getting ready in the morning because I am worried about how other people will view me. I lose sleep by replaying memories in my head over and over again. I waste so many hours of my day on pointless crap.

My anxiety stops me from speaking my mind. When I have something to add in class or in a group conversation, I will wait for an opening to speak instead of jumping in at random. But before I'm able to say my piece, the topic will change and I will have lost my chance to explain. I will have missed my opportunity.

My anxiety stops me from chasing after the people I want. When I have feelings for someone, I will wait for them to come to me. I will stare at them from across a room and hope that they approach. I will stare at my phone for hours on end and hope that they send a text. I will do nothing to show my interest and hope they guess how I feel.

My anxiety stops me from leaving my house. It keeps me attached to the one place where I know I am safe. I spend most of my day on the couch, in my bed, or digging through the fridge. I ignore texts and put off answering emails. I isolate myself and then complain about being lonely.

My anxiety stops me from meeting new people. I am more relaxed when I know what I am going to get, so I avoid new places. I avoid different experiences. I try to stay within my comfort zone as much as possible.

My anxiety stops me from feeling confident. I avoid getting my hair and nails done professionally because I'm afraid of interacting with the staff. I avoid wearing cute clothing because I'm worried that I won't be able to pull it off. I avoid flirting with people because I'm convinced that I will make a fool of myself.

My anxiety stops me from enjoying the moment. I am either living in the past or predicting the future. I am either counting down the hours until something I dread starts or until something I enjoy ends. I am never happy right where I am. My mind is always miles away.

My anxiety stops me from finding happiness. It convinces me that I am alone. It lies to me about my worth. It makes me feel like there is something wrong with me like I am not doing enough, like I am never going to be enough.

There are so many things my anxiety has stopped me from doing in the past, but I am not going to let the trend continue. I am not going to let anxiety stop me from living my best life.

44

33 Lies That Anxiety Tells Me (That I Should Stop Believing)

1. I am not pretty enough.
   2. I am not funny enough.
   3. I am not *enough*.
   4. No one wants me around.
   5. My friends secretly hate me.
   6. I am probably annoying them.
   7. No one understands what I am going through.
   8. There is something seriously wrong with me.
   9. No one is ever going to fall in love with me.
   10. There is no point in even trying.
   11. I am going to chase everyone away.
   12. I am insane.
   13. I can't hold a simple conversation.
   14. I am going to embarrass myself in front of everyone.
   15. I should just stay home.
   16. I am going to get fired.
   17. I am going to fail my class.
   18. I am going to get cheated on.
   19. I am never going to fall asleep.

20. Things are going too well lately.
21. Something horrible is going to happen soon.
22. I can't tell anyone what I'm really thinking.
23. They are all laughing at me.
24. They are all staring at me.
25. They are all judging me.
26. I sound like an idiot.
27. I don't want to deal with this anymore.
28. I can't handle this.
29. I am going to die of embarrassment.
30. I hate myself.
31. I am a failure.
32. Things are never going to change.
33. I am never going to beat my anxiety.

45

33 Things To Tell Myself The Next Time My Anxiety Hits

1. I am stronger than my anxiety.
2. This feeling is going to pass.
3. Everything is going to be okay soon.
4. I am allowed to feel this way.
5. I am not overreacting.
6. I am not being dramatic.
7. I should not feel ashamed.
8. I am not the only one who feels this way.
9. This is nothing to be embarrassed about.
10. I shouldn't believe the lies my anxiety tells me.
11. There is nothing wrong with me.
12. These feelings aren't my fault.
13. I am strong enough to handle this.
14. I have gotten through this before and will again.
15. Nothing bad is going to happen.
16. There are so many people who love me.
17. And I love myself.
18. I need to trust myself.
19. I need to focus on my breathing.

20. I need to breathe in deep.

21. And I need to release that breath.

22. I am not going to die over this.

23. My life is not going to be ruined over this.

24. My anxiety is only a part of me.

25. My anxiety does not define me.

26. I forgive myself for feeling this way.

27. No one else is judging me as hard as I am judging myself.

28. There are other people who understand what I am going through.

29. I am not as alone as I feel right now.

30. In fact, I am *never* alone.

31. This really sucks, but it will end soon.

32. Even if my anxiety comes back again, I will be okay.

33. I *am* okay.

46

Without Anxiety, I Would Be A Totally Different Person

Without anxiety, I wouldn't have such close friends. My anxiety has driven certain people away, but it has brought other people closer to me. The kind of people who I can count on. The kind of people who refuse to walk away when things get hard. The kind of people who deserve a permanent place in my life.

My anxiety has helped me see how much they care about me because they have stayed by my side through it all. They never gave up on me even when I gave up on myself. They stayed through the times when I was cranky and insecure and angry with the world. They even stayed when I went missing in action for a few days. They never let our friendship die because I meant too much to them, and I am so thankful to have them in my life.

Without anxiety, I wouldn't appreciate the good things in my life as deeply. Flirting would come easy for me, so I wouldn't realize how lucky I was to have people who are interested in me. Raising my hand in class would be no big deal and neither would be going on job interviews, so I wouldn't be as careful about what I said and how I came across. I wouldn't take life so seriously.

But I do suffer from anxiety, so interviewing for my job was a big step for me. Graduating was a big step for me. Going out on a first date was a big step for me. Without anxiety, I might have taken those milestones for granted. I might not have cherished them as they were meant to be cherished. I might not have realized how lucky I am to have such exciting opportunities.

Without anxiety, I wouldn't be the person I am today. I would have a completely different personality. I would have a completely different group of friends. I would have a completely different lifestyle. I used to want those things to change, but now I am realizing that I am happy the way everything has turned out. I am happy with everything that I have created for myself.

I have friends who would do anything for me. I have a job that I am proud to be working. I am making my own money. I am creating my own happiness. I am living my own life.

Without anxiety, I wouldn't be such a strong person. I wouldn't know the extent of what I am capable of achieving. I wouldn't have to push myself as hard. I wouldn't have to try as much. I wouldn't have to do so many things that I am scared of doing.

My anxiety pushes me out of my comfort zone every single day. It makes living harder than it needs to be. It causes me extra, unnecessary stress. But I have survived all of that. I have persisted. I am still here and I am doing better than ever before. I am happier than ever before.

My anxiety hasn't made me weaker. It has made me stronger.

47

The Strongest Girls Are The Girls With Anxiety

She's strong because she's in a constant battle with her anxiety. It's telling her that she's weak. That she shouldn't speak up. That she shouldn't get out of bed.

Some days, she listens to everything that voice tells her. But other days, she finds the power to ignore it. She finds the strength to leave her room. To socialize. To smile.

She's strong because she shows up, even when she's shaking. She speaks, even when it's with a cracked voice. She keeps breathing, even when those breaths are shaky.

It would be easy for her to cancel plans with her friends, turn down dates, skip class, call in sick from work — and sometimes, she does. Sometimes, the idea of being around people is too much for her to handle.

But most of the time, she does what she has to do. She switches off her alarm. She showers. She dresses. And then she gets shit done.

Of course, she gets distracted throughout the day. The tiniest thing can send her mind spinning. A text from someone she didn't expect to hear from. An email she isn't quite sure how to answer. A strange look from one of her coworkers or crushes.

She suffers from constant self-consciousness, but she pushes past it. She ignores the way she thinks everyone is looking at her, judging her, and she forces herself to be productive. She forces herself to focus on what's important.

She refuses to let anxiety control her life. She won't let her dark thoughts eclipse the positive ones. She's motivated to be the best person she can be.

At times, her anxiety makes her feel weak. Lesser. Like she doesn't deserve to be in the same room as people that can talk to strangers as if they've known each other for years.

But even though she feels inferior, that's far from the truth. She's a warrior. A badass. Why can't she see that?

She tries so hard. She puts in so much effort. And she's gotten so far.

Some people rarely venture outside of their comfort zone — but she's outside of her comfort zone every damn day. She's either worried about what to say or what to wear or where to park. She's never relaxed. She's always on edge.

That's why she's always learning. Always growing. Every second of every day.

Sure, there are times when she suffers from setbacks. When she doesn't say a single word for hours. When she stays in her pajamas and puts off showering.

But there are other times when she finds the courage to speak her mind. When she surprises herself with how brave she can be.

She probably doesn't realize it yet, but girls with anxiety are the strongest girls in the world because they never have a minute of peace. Because they're always struggling — and they're always winning.

48

I Refuse To Let Anxiety Ruin My Life

I refuse to let anxiety ruin my life. I refuse to listen to the nagging thoughts in the back of my mind, telling me that I will never amount to anything, that I am ugly and untalented, that the people I consider close friends are only hanging out with me because they feel bad for me.

I refuse to hide away out of fear. I refuse to believe the lies that anxiety whispers in my ears. I refuse to give anxiety unlimited power over me.

There will continue to be days when I turn down party invitations because I cannot handle the intricacies of social interaction. There will be other days when I find the strength to attend a party, but spend the entire time locked inside of the bathroom, counting down the minutes until I can leave. But, even though it might not feel like it now, there will be days when I walk through the front door with my head high and my head clear. When I have a fun time with my friends without worrying about anything at all. When the only thing I'm thinking about is how much I love my life.

There will continue to be days when I call in sick from work because I can't bring myself to get out of bed and swap my pajamas for a pantsuit. There will be other days when I drive myself to the office on time and get all my work done, but don't say a word the entire day because I feel like everyone hates me. But, even though it might not feel like it now, there will be days when I impress my boss. When I talk to my coworkers without stuttering. When I feel like I am doing something meaningful. When I feel like I am exactly where I belong.

There will continue to be days when I ignore the urge to text the person I have strong feelings for because I can't think of anything clever to say and don't want to be a bother. There will be other days when I initiate a conversation with them but chicken out when it comes time to asking them to hang out in person. But, even though it might not feel like it now, there will be days when I make the first move. When I go out on dates. When I look good and feel even better.

There will continue to be days when my anxiety cripples me when it keeps me locked inside its jaws. There will be other days when I feel anxiety's pull but manage to ignore it, for the most part, to look normal to everyone around me while I'm dying inside. But, even though it might not feel like it now, there will be days when I battle my anxiety and come out victorious. There will be days when my anxiety finally loses.

I refuse to let anxiety ruin my life. I refuse to lose hope in myself. And I refuse to lose hope in you.

49

I Am Slowly Learning My Anxiety Is Nothing To Be Ashamed Of

I am slowly learning that I am not the only person in the world who struggles with anxiety. There are a million other people who are just like me, who deal with the same stressful issues. I am not as alone as I feel. I do not have to keep my problems to myself out of fear that no one else will understand. I do not have to continue pretending because my anxiety is nothing to be ashamed of having. It is not a secret that I have to keep to myself.

I am slowly learning that anxiety is not going to cause me to stay single forever. It is not going to chase everyone else away. There are people out there who will love me through my anxiety. People who will be happy to hold me close and squeeze when my thoughts get out of control. People who will not run away at the first sign of a panic attack. People who will be there for me, who will stick by my side, no matter what my brain puts me through.

I am slowly learning that my anxious thoughts are not

always true. Just because I *think* that someone is staring at me or judging the way that I look does not mean that is the reality of the situation. My brain can play tricks on me. My brain can convince me that everyone secretly hates me when in reality, no one is that concerned with me. They are too busy thinking about themselves.

I am slowly learning to accept my anxiety. Wasting my time whining about it will not do me any good. Instead of claiming that life is unfair and wondering *why me*, I need to discover coping methods that will work for me. I need to practice deep breathing exercises. I need to alter my diet and get more sleep. I need to find a therapist that I can trust. I need to figure out what helps me cope with my anxiety best because different things work for different people.

I am slowly learning that suffering from anxiety does not make me weak. Struggling to socialize does not make me weird. Overthinking does not make me psycho. If anything, my anxiety makes me strong, because it takes bravery to get up every morning and face the day. It takes courage to speak up when I would rather stay quiet. It takes guts to survive in this world.

I am slowly learning that I cannot let anxiety hold me back any longer. If I want to attend a party, I should go even if I end up leaving early. If I want to apply for my dream job, I should send in an application even if I will obsess over my resume weeks. If I want to live my life to the fullest, I need to leave my comfort zone even though it's scary.

I am slowly learning that anxiety is not going to ruin my life. It is only going to make my successes feel even sweeter because I spent so long doubting myself. Because I never realized how much I was capable of achieving.

About the Author

Holly Riordan grew up on Long Island, New York where she earned her English degree from Stony Brook University. Now, she writes about anxiety, almost relationships, and the loss of loved ones for Thought Catalog.

ALSO BY HOLLY RIORDAN:

Severe(d)

Badass Broken Girls

If You Were Still Alive

THOUGHT
CATALOG
Books

THOUGHT
CATALOG
Books

Thought Catalog Books is a publishing house owned by The
Thought & Expression Company, an independent media group
based in Brooklyn, NY. Founded in 2010, we are committed
to facilitating thought and expression. We exist to help people
become better communicators and listeners in order to engen-
der a more exciting, attentive, and imaginative world.

Visit us on the web at
www.thoughtcatalogbooks.com and *www.collective.world*.

Made in the USA
Monee, IL
30 July 2021

74573234R00080